THE STORY OF JERICHO

SOME BOOKS BY

PROFESSOR J. GARSTANG

THE LAND OF THE HITTITES

THE HITTITE EMPIRE

THE FOUNDATIONS OF BIBLE HISTORY : JOSHUA JUDGES

THE HERITAGE OF SOLOMON

An Artist's Impression of the Fourth City of Jericho.

Frontispiece

THE STORY OF JERICHO

BY

JOHN GARSTANG

AND

J. B. E. GARSTANG

With Illustrations

LONDON

HODDER & STOUGHTON LIMITED

First printed . . . 1940

Made and Printed in Great Britain for Hodder & Stoughton, Limited by C. Tinling & Co., Ltd., Liverpool, London and Prescot.

TO OUR FRIEND

" PHYTHIAN "

The Rev. W. J. Phythian-Adams, D.S.O., M.C., D.D.
Canon of Carlisle
Chaplain to H.M. the King

CONTENTS

ILLUSTRATIONS

Frontispiece : An artist's impression of the Fourth City of Jericho.

PLATES

(L. *indicates a line drawing*)

ILLUSTRATIONS

MAPS

FIGURES IN THE TEXT

ILLUSTRATIONS

AUTHORS' PREFACE

IT has been our first endeavour in preparing this volume to present the archæological facts faithfully to the reader, and not to offend his intelligence by omitting technical details, when these may help to establish in his mind the validity of our conclusions. This applies particularly to descriptions or archæological evidences bearing upon the Bible narrative, about which it is desirable that the reader should have full opportunity of judging for himself.

Throughout the six seasons devoted to the researches described in these pages the expedition was mostly staffed by students and voluntary helpers, the list of whose names varied from time to time and is accordingly rather long. Bulos Effendi el Araj, as Clerk of Works and Surveyor, Mrs. John Garstang, as camp and laboratory supervisor, and Mrs. Peter Fleming (née Meroë Garstang) as secretary, registrar and field assistant, worked however each year.

In the earlier stages good help was given in the field by Mr. Donald McCown, Mr. Ted McCown and the Bishop of Rochester ; and the late Madame Krausse-Marquet (née Judith Krausse) also assisted with registration, records and cataloguing, a heavy task while work was proceeding in the tombs.

Mrs. Geoffrey Jellicoe (née Susan Pares) also gave valued service during that time of pressure as Director's secretary. Later Mrs. Robert Gurney, Mr. Thomas Hodgkin and Mr. E. J. M. Buxton assisted in the field work ; and our esteemed friend Mr. G. M. FitzGerald relieved the Director of much detailed supervision in the rôle of "Director's friend". In the last season Mr. Alan Rowe became field supervisor ; and Mr. I. Ben-Dor, who studied the Neolithic pottery on the spot, contributed an illuminative description of it to our reports.

As architects Major Key and Mr. William Buffum at the outset, then Mr. William Gadd, and in later years Mr. John Richmond all worked unsparingly ; and together with Bulos Effendi they provided the surveys which form the basis of many illustrations in this book. The photography was mostly done by the Director, with the help in different years of Mr. Harold Falconer and Dr. O. R. Gurney.

Mrs. Dennis Payne (née Joan Crowfoot) as expert in charge of the prehistoric section, assisted for some time by Miss Veronica Seton Williams, showed throughout meticulous care and method in classifying the large number of flint implements, and her scholarly exposition of the results of our investigations in this new field has gained a permanent place in prehistoric studies. The scarabs, 181 in number, were also examined and reported on by an expert, Professor P. E. Newberry, who visited Jericho specially for this purpose.

The excavations were made under the ægis of

the Institute of Archæology of the University of Liverpool, in the *Annals* of which a summary of results was published yearly from 1930 to 1936. The cost of the work was borne partly by private subscribers, headed each year by Sir Charles Marston, who was substantially backed up at various times by the late Lord Melchett and Mr. Davies Bryan; and partly by the University Museums of Oxford, Cambridge and Glasgow, and the civic Museums of Birmingham, Liverpool and Leeds, with the consistent support of the Musées du Louvre, Paris, and the collaboration for several years of the Musée du Cinquantenaire at Brussels. The specimens allowed to us by the Palestine Government were distributed among these bodies, the most complete series being that of the Hunterian Museum in Glasgow.

We thank sincerely Mrs. Robert Gurney, Mrs. J. B. E. Garstang and Canon Phythian-Adams for their help and advice in the writing and construction of this book; and also Miss Mabel Ratcliffe, who at the Institute of Archæology in Liverpool has worked untiringly for several years upon the complex records of our work, and has prepared our plates and drawings for publication. Her "artist's impression" of the City before its fall which forms our frontispiece is all the more worthy of attention.

NOVEMBER 28, 1939.

Chronological Outline of The Story of Jericho

Stone Age

4500-3000 B.C.	Settlements of the Neolithic Period.

Bronze Age

3000-2500 B.C.	City I :	Babylonian Influence.
2500-2000 B.C.	City II :	Babylonian Influence.
1900-1750 B.C.	City III :	Canaanite.
1750-1600 B.C.	City III :	Hyksos Stronghold.
1580-1480 B.C.	City IV :	Egyptian Domination
1480-1400 B.C.	City IV :	Egyptian Suzerainty.
1400-1385 B.C.	Destruction of City IV (Joshua vi).	

Iron Age

1285-1150 B.C.	Blockhouse and Cremation Pit.
900- 700 B.C.	City V : (I Kings, xvi, 34).

CHAPTER I

INTRODUCTORY

JERICHO AND THE ANCIENT WORLD

CHAPTER I

OF the many stirring episodes narrated in the Old Testament, probably none has so impressed itself upon the popular imagination as the description in the Book of Joshua of the fall of Jericho. Indeed, were it not for that narrative, the place would hardly have been remembered. Shorn by political and economic changes of any special interest, it might have remained to this day a meaningless heap of mud and ruins, one of the hundreds of similar " Tells " which dot the landscape of Palestine, Syria and Mesopotamia, wherever mud is available for making bricks.

The graphic description of Jericho in the Bible has now been amplified by an examination of the ruins themselves ; for remains of the walled city have been found and traced beneath the debris of later times. It was destroyed as all know by the incoming Israelites, and the Biblical narrative defines the stages of its annihilation. In the Sixth Chapter of the Book of Joshua (vv. 20, 21 and 24) we read :

> " *The wall fell down flat* (or *in a heap*), *so that the people went up into the city, every man straight before him. . . . And they utterly destroyed all that was in the city. And they burnt the city with fire and all that was therein.*"

These episodes are confirmed in all material particulars: the fallen walls have been laid bare, while the burning of demolished buildings is found to have been general and so conspicuous as to suggest a deliberate holocaust. Again we read in verse 26:

> "*And Joshua charged them with an oath at that time saying, Cursed be the man before the Lord that riseth up and buildeth this city Jericho.*"

From a later passage in the 1st Book of Kings (xvi, 34) we may infer that no attempt was made to rebuild Jericho until the reign of Ahab about 900 B.C.; and our excavations have in fact proved that after its destruction the walled city was not reconstructed, nor was the site more than partially inhabited, for about 500 years.

But the revelations of the spade do not end there. They show that the city destroyed in the 14th century B.C. occupied the site of one of the oldest known communities of Palestine, indeed one of the earliest settlements of man found anywhere. It could claim already an almost continuous life history of some 5,000 years, during which it had shared in the gradual evolution of human culture through the successive stages of the Stone, Copper and Bronze Ages. Research has shown that progress, wherever unrestricted, followed much the same sequence, though varying with the special conditions of each area; but to some of the early stages of development Jericho made its own signal contributions, notably the invention of pottery and experiments in plastic art; and each subsequent stage has disclosed features of special interest and character.

In this book we shall attempt to trace in simple outline the story of Jericho through these successive Ages, to examine the circumstances of its fall, and to show how and to what extent it had shared in the origins and growth of the civilization of the Holy Land which has contributed so greatly to the enlightenment of man.

In the first place let us meet the natural enquiry, why Jericho in particular should have become the home of the earliest community in Palestine—for what special reason or purpose man settled there first and not elsewhere. The answer involves several considerations.

The most striking feature about Jericho is its situation in the Jordan Rift. This is part of the natural "fault" which runs from the Sea of Galilee down to the Dead Sea and beyond. The Jordan Valley, properly so called, ought really to be distinguished from the Rift, which is not a valley in the ordinary sense of the word, but a deep and wide chasm, ten or twelve miles across, down the middle of which the river winds in its own alluvial bed. At the lower end of this Rift, about five miles west of the river, some 500 feet above the waters of the Dead Sea but still 800 feet below normal sea-level, stood ancient Jericho. When we recall that the mountains of Judæa (on which some twenty miles distant stands Jerusalem) rise 4,000 feet above Jericho, and that the hill country of Moab forms an equally high plateau immediately to the east beyond the Jordan, we can understand why Jericho enjoys semi-tropical vegetation. The hills on either side not only shelter the bottoms from the prevailing winds but reflect the sun's heat downwards, so that the rift-valley in summer seems like a boiling cauldron, with the temperature as high as 130 degrees in the shade. Such heat is of course

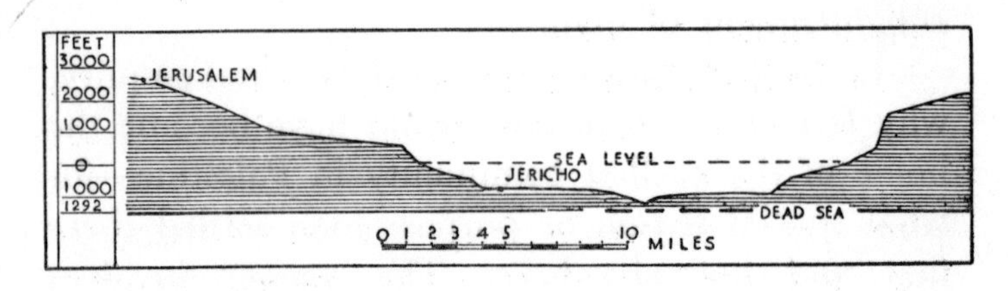

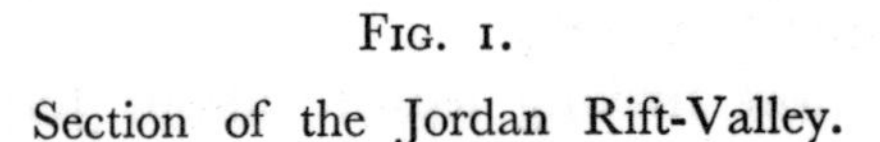

Fig. 1.

Section of the Jordan Rift-Valley.

very enervating, and saps the vigour of life from man and beast; but in the winter, while Jerusalem is mostly cold and sometimes under snow, Jericho enjoys the climate of a good English summer: bananas are ripe for eating in December.

The actual site of ancient Jericho was from the first determined by the presence of a bountiful spring of water, which later became famous as Elisha's Fountain. In a country where most towns rely for their water on storage tanks beneath the houses, where rivers and streams are few and far between, and even the largest of them like the Kishon may run dry during the summer months, such a spring, flowing as it does at about 1,000

PLATE I

Some Views at Jericho

PLATE II

THE ANCIENT SITE OF JERICHO UNDER EXCAVATION

gallons a minute with but little variation, could never fail to attract settlers. The district is served, moreover, by a second and equally abundant spring which rises at the foot of the western hills, whence its waters are led down by canals to supplement the supplies already available for cultivation. Such a water supply, though naturally restricted and insufficient for a city of any great size, was at any rate more than enough for the needs of small primitive communities and for the city that later developed on the site. The rest of the rift-valley is largely sterile, and even by the banks of the Jordan cultivation is rendered difficult by the sourness of the ground and the normal depth of that river below its banks. It is true that at certain times, as when the snows melt on Mount Hermon, the Jordan overflows and advantage may be taken of this phenomenon; but it is not extensive or general, as for instance is the annual rising of the Nile.

To the people of a barren land, where life was difficult, Jericho must have appeared at all times a haven of contentment. Shepherds who lived in the bleak hill country of Palestine and Moab might well look down with envy upon the walled town with its semi-tropical oasis. Travellers and merchants who were obliged to pass that way would be tempted to stop or to return with their families and belongings; for here was a land of palm-trees, fruit gardens and corn, where hard work was well rewarded and beneficent nature provided everything necessary for life and even more. Small wonder, then, that primitive man was attracted early to this site, and that through the ages successive migratory groups strove for its possession. Long after the old city had fallen, Herod the Great established here his winter palace, and employed the skill of Roman engineers to lead down more water in aqueducts from the hills, so extending the cultivated area further to the south.

In addition to its exceptionally good supply of water, the importance of Jericho in early times was also enhanced by its position in relation to nature's trackways in that part of the world. It controlled one of the permanent fords across the Jordan, and thus became the meeting place of several trade routes coming from the East, which in their turn branched out westwards from Jericho towards Bethel and Shechem in the north, to Jerusalem directly west and to Hebron in the south. Another important though less familiar track led northward by the Jordan Rift.

This central position of Jericho upon so many trade routes, though perhaps not explaining the original settlement, profoundly influenced its subsequent life history. It will be interesting therefore to follow up some of them and glance at the culture of those areas with which it was thus brought into communication.

To begin with the West: the tracks through Jerusalem and Hebron, which in later times linked Jericho with Egypt by way of the northern deserts of Sinai, do not seem to have been opened for trade during the prehistoric period. This is at first sight surprising; for civilization in the Nile valley, as in Jericho, was already well advanced in the late Neolithic period. Each area seems, however, to have nurtured a distinct culture, and there has been found no certain trace of direct contact between the two until the beginning of the Early Bronze Age. This is shown by evidence from our excavations to have been more or less contemporary with the establishment of the first dynasty of Kings in Egypt (about 3,000 B.C.). It is to be noted also that the history of cities on the highlands immediately to the west of Jericho (such as Shechem, Bethel and Jerusalem) began about that time, so that in earlier epochs the deserts of Sinai seem to have formed too great a barrier for primitive man to cross for trading purposes. The provision of drinking water for a ten days' journey was no doubt beyond his resources. Even though he may have possessed water skins, trained animals would have been required to carry them; while the earliest handmade water-vessels of pottery were altogether too fragile to support the journey. None the less, communication was certainly open in Neolithic times as far as the desert borders, since settlements with similar characteristics have been found in the Wady Gerar beyond Gaza, and surface deposits of similar stone implements have been picked up elsewhere in the south.

The track which links Jericho with the North by way of the Jordan Valley, though developed in Roman times, never seems to have become popular as a trade route, and even to-day it is largely deserted and in places difficult. Probably caravans and traders were deterred from adopting it by the great heat during most part of the year in the sunken rift, and by its desolate nature, which left them at the mercy of raiding tribes and brigands from the hills. The distance from Jericho to Beisan by this road is about fifty miles, and for the first thirty-five of these there is found no trace of ancient habitation. It emerges from the enclosed valley at Beisan, whence natural routes branch in all directions. Excavations have shown that the origins of this settlement also go back to prehistoric times, and that some of its earliest products are directly comparable with Late Stone Age specimens from Jericho. Beyond Beisan the valley road continues northwards, skirting the western shore of the Sea of Galilee, through the Huleh Basin, and so on past the foot of Hermon. It links eastward with Damascus, westward with the coasts of Tyre and Sidon, and northwards with the old site of Homs whence also there is ready access to the sea.

A coastal road extends the northerly link as far as Ras Shamra, a place which has become famous of late through the discovery of tablets in which mention is made of the northern tribes of Israel, as well as possible allusions to Ashdod in the Philistine plain and the desert area of the Negeb further south. These references belong, of course, to historic times ; but they indicate an established line of communication. It is therefore of special interest to learn that excavations in deep levels of that site have revealed traces of a Late Stone Age culture having something in common with that of Jericho.

Ras Shamra seems to mark the limit of Jericho's relationships in prehistoric times. Further north Syria came within the influence of the more advanced contemporary civilizations of Mesopotamia, which may be traced even around the bend of the coast as far westward as Mersin at the outlet of the Cilician plain. An ancient site located there of recent years rivals Jericho in the antiquity of its origins. But in this case, again, we learn how complete was the isolation of these old Neolithic societies. For as we examine and compare the deeper levels of the Stone Age settlements at Mersin and Jericho layer by layer, we find nothing to indicate any original relationship between the two. Something in the earliest pottery of Mersin does suggest a possible contact with pre-dynastic Egypt, but that would not necessarily argue a land route through Syria, much less by way of Jericho. Asia Minor then, no less than Egypt, must be regarded as having remained all through the Stone Age beyond the horizon of the settlers by the Jordan.

For various reasons the connexions of Jericho with the East were more favoured and in general more effective. Though the progress of cultural influence might be slow, there were three main routes by which it might travel from that direction : all three pass through Amman, the Biblical Rabbath-Ammon, which lies eastward from Jericho at a distance of about sixty miles.

One of these routes communicates with the south-lands, where lie Kerak (the Biblical Kir of Moab), perched upon an isolated hill in the middle of rugged surroundings ; and further south Petra (conceivably to be identified with Kadesh-barnea),[1] nestling within the security of its natural ramparts. The route leads on southward towards the head of the Gulf of Akaba. Though most of the country between Amman and this terminus is poor, and produced little that contributed to human progress, it formed none the less the goal of numerous caravan routes from central and southern Arabia, along which through all time has come a steady influx of Arab traders as well as nomads seeking water and pasture in time of drought. Very occasionally the tracks have been traversed by armed hordes having the Holy Land as their objective, and with Jericho as the first obstacle in their path.

The second of these routes spreads out in several directions through the partial desert that borders upon the ploughlands of Transjordan. One of the best known of these tracks bends south-east to Jôf by way of the Wady Sirhan. In the Biblical story of Gideon it was already known as " the Way of the Nomads," a name which has aptly described its significance through all ages ; for as recently as A.D. 1927 it was by this route that the Wahabis attempted their invasion of Palestine.

The third route, closely concerned with our story, leads northward from Amman by the edge

[1] cf. Phythian-Adams : *The Call of Israel*, p. 69.

of the deserts, so avoiding the steeper river valleys descending to the Jordan. It passes by way of Damascus, whence the way lies open via Palmyra to several crossings of the Euphrates, the nearest being at Mari, and the most popular higher up at El Zor. Through these doors passed the main trade routes that linked Palestine and the Jordan valley with the old civilized societies by the lower Euphrates and the Tigris.

For Jericho the connexions thus established with Mesopotamia and Babylonia were all important. As will be seen in a later chapter, Babylonian influence became visible, culturally at least, at the beginning of the historic period, about 3000 B.C.; and it endured as the dominant element for a full thousand years. But the political changes which ensued by no means severed this eastern link. On the contrary, the historic relations with Mesopotamia, reflected in the legends of the patriarchs, are now revivified by the identity of their social laws and practices with some of those described in written records discovered at Nuzi, to the south of Nineveh, the centre of a district readily identified with Arphaxad (Arpachshad), the classical Arpachitis. Scholars long ago pointed out that "Ur of the Chaldees," the home of the Abrahamic family (Genesis xi, 28, 31), might even be a misreading of "Arphaxad".[1] However that may be, the stories of the traditional patriarchal movement towards the Jordan can now be readily fitted as episodes within a known historical frame-

[1] cf. Phythian-Adams: *The Fulness of Israel*, p. 65.

work. The connexions between Jericho and the Mesopotamian area thus become alive with reality. But this is not all: they seem to have had a much earlier origin.

In the Biblical narrative of the Flood, after the landing of the children of Noah among the mountains of Ararat (Genesis viii, 4 and ix, 18) one branch of the Semites (the sons of Shem) became identified with Arphaxad (Genesis x, 21–24), and it was from this branch that Abraham and Lot were descended (Genesis xi, 16–27).

> "*And the sons of Noah that went forth from the Ark were Shem, and Ham, and Japheth: and Ham is the father of Canaan.*"
>
> "*And unto Shem, the father of all the children of Eber, the elder brother of Japheth, to him also were children born. The sons of Shem: Elam, and Asshur, and Arphaxad, and Lud, and Aram. And Arphaxad begat Shelah; and Shelah begat Eber.*"

There is no doubt that these records preserve time-honoured traditions which hark back to a remoter past, to the beginnings in fact of human activities in this area, after a devastating flood. Now researches of the last decade have revealed traces of the oldest settlements of man in this part of the ancient world, and they are not without direct bearing on our story. The district to the north of Nineveh extending towards Mount Ararat, as well as northern Mesopotamia and the western foothills, was inhabited during the fourth millennium B.C. by people whose arts and crafts bore a distinctive character, though limited in range. The Period is called "Chalcolithic" because implements and tools were made not only of stone as in the earlier Age, but also of metal, the discovery of which marked a beginning of new standards for civilization. Each stage in this progress towards a higher cultural development is now named, as is usual, after the excavated site where its products were first discovered. Thus the oldest and most striking of these culture-stages is called Halafian, after the name of a site called Tell Halaf; but more instructive remains of this stage have been found in other places, notably at Arpachiyah and Tepe Gawra to the north of Nineveh, and also at Samarra in the south. Its influence was by no means confined to the vicinity of Nineveh, but ranged widely over northern Mesopotamia, and to the west of the Euphrates in Northern Syria. It has left its traces in that direction on the sea coast at Ras Shamra already mentioned, and even as far westward as Mersin.

The distinctive features of this Age are the excellence and variety of its painted pottery, and the astonishing development of its architecture both in principle and in construction. The city at Mersin was girt with a stout defensive wall, pierced with apertures for the use of archers. At both Tepe Gawra and Mersin large houses were built upon a common plan in which a narrow central court open to the sky was flanked on either hand by a series of rooms. Somewhat late in this period the walls and floors of houses at Tepe Gawra are found to have been plastered and covered with a red wash, and use was made of the pilaster for constructive purposes. It is significant that at Jericho, where also architecture developed early, exactly similar details of construction appear in certain buildings of the Late Stone Age. These points of contact may seem slight, but such features are exceptional, and this fact lends them strength. Not only do they suggest that the people of Jericho were still in a Neolithic stage of civilization while more advanced societies further east had developed a Chalcolithic culture; but they also enable us to assign a tentative date to the origins of our site. The Middle or Second Phase of the Late Stone Age at Jericho would seem from these indications to fall in the Halafian Period, between 4000 and 3500 B.C.

We may conveniently sum up at this stage the broad cultural contacts of Jericho in a form which will at the same time explain some of the archæological terms of which we must make occasional use throughout this book, together with round dates. Each Age may be further subdivided into culture-phases, as shown in the Chronological chart on p. 178 of the Appendix.

	Historic :	
Late Bronze Age .	Egyptian upon Hyksos .	1600-1400 B.C.
Middle Bronze Age	Hyksos upon Canaanite	2000-1600 B.C.
Early Bronze Age .	Babylonian . .	3000-2000 B.C.
	Prehistoric :	
Late Stone Age .	Local Neolithic : (Three phases)	4500-3000 B.C.
Middle Stone Age .	Mesolithic Period (?) (doubtful)	Before 5000 B.C.
Early Stone Age .	Paleolithic Period	Not represented.

CHAPTER II

EXCAVATIONS AND DISCOVERIES

CHAPTER II

"HOW did you know where to dig?" This is a question often asked; and the answer has two aspects, firstly how to locate the site, and secondly how to set about the digging. With regard to the first of these we have to acknowledge our debt to generations of pioneer explorers and archæologists, who have already examined much of the ancient East and identified most of the famous sites in the light of historic objects or of inscriptions found upon the spot. The names of Layard, Newton and Rawlinson must remain ever associated with such early discoveries in Mesopotamia; as in our special field do those of the first workers for the Palestine Exploration Fund, Warren, Conder and many others, including the great Kitchener who helped to map the country. There was little difficulty, indeed, with some places, such as Jerusalem, Hebron, Gaza, Acre and Bethshan, where the names have survived and local remains bear witness to their antiquity. Many such cities have now a definite place upon standard maps of the Ancient East; and the relative positions of doubtful sites can sometimes be located provisionally, by inference from the records and investigation of the ground.

But the actual identification of unknown cities

presents special problems. If historical records, such as the New Testament, allude to a Greek or Roman city, then the explorer first searches for remains of these civilizations in the locality indicated. He must next make sure, however, that such columns of temple or forum, and other architectural fragments or sculpture as he may find, really belong to the locality ; for even an inscribed tomb-stone may have been brought from elsewhere as building material in a later age. But a mile-stone or other inscribed monument bearing a place-name, and found *in situ*, would provide a definite clue from which the position of the city might be fixed with certainty.

The conditions, however, may offer further complications ; for if, as with Jericho, we are looking for something much more ancient, the sites are not always self-evident, and the nature of the antiquities characteristic of the period in question may not be so generally known : in particular there is not likely to be any local inscription to tell its story. Still the principle of putting two and two together remains the same. The ancient site will probably be marked by a prominent mound or *Tell*, such as those which dot the landscape of the Near East in favourable areas. In shape they resemble, but are much larger than, the long barrows or burial mounds of this country. Travellers through Bulgaria see many larger examples of such from the railway train. The old city mounds of western Asia are larger still, the smallest covering six acres of ground, the average twice that area.

PLATE III

The Pottery Bench and Two Repaired Vessels

PLATE IV

THE BEGINNING OF OUR EXCAVATIONS

They rise usually 30 to 40 feet above the ground, and may be twice that height. If deserted before the Roman era, as many were owing to the advent of malaria or changes of economic conditions, they are commonly flat topped, or they may present a high shoulder towards the sea breeze, marking (as it often proves) the position of the chief building lying in ruins. An essential characteristic is that for the most part they will prove on investigation to be almost wholly artificial—the accumulation of ruined townships built mostly of mud bricks which in past ages arose there in succession, each standing upon the debris of its predecessor. Disintegrated bricks were not worth removal; and so such mounds grew age after age, until some final catastrophe arrested further occupation. The antiquities found in them or on their slopes may be limited to small potsherds, but these the modern science of archæology has taught us to study on other sites already excavated, and so to learn their periods. It is in this way that an ancient city may be recognized and its antiquity can be attested. But how can it be identified if there are no direct local indications? In that case we must work inwards from outside sources.

The solution of such a problem is usually a matter of logical reasoning, rather like the processes of a detective's methods and all the more fascinating for that reason. It is rare nowadays to be able to localize and identify a lost site famous in history, for most have already been discovered. The thrill is all the greater when it does happen, and we may be allowed to illustrate this aspect of our enquiry from the discovery of Hazor, which, like Jericho, is said to have been burnt by Joshua—the closing episode of his great military career.

Hazor is described in the Bible as the head of a league of Canaanitish cities, which included well known places like Bethshan, Taanach and Megiddo in the plain of Esdrælon, others such as Achshaph and Sidon near the coast, and some to the east of Jordan. It must have been a chariotry centre :

> " *They went out, they and all their hosts with them, much people . . . with horses and chariots very many.*" (Joshua xi, 4.)

It was therefore to be looked for in the plains. Now a study of a contoured or relief map of Palestine will show that all these allied places are connected by roads which meet in the plain of the Huleh Basin, where to-day a customs-post actually controls their junction.

It was with these considerations in mind that the writer of these lines set out from the north end of the Sea of Galilee one early morning in the autumn of 1927 to try to locate the spot—early to avoid the heat of noon, and because in flat-land shadows are all-important to such investigations. By seven o'clock the customs-post had been passed by a couple of miles, when a hill at a sudden turn of the road presented an excellent observation point. Twenty minutes later, from the top, there loomed up the whole outline of a vast camp enclosure reaching northwards from the hill itself which formed its southern boundary. It was a thousand yards from north to south : its ramparts of beaten earth were sixty feet in height ; the corners were rounded and protected with great rocks, all thrown into vivid relief by the morning sun. Prodigious and all unexpected as it was there could be no illusion : yet the Kitchener map marked it as a natural feature. If only the potsherds conformed ! . . . a mad scamper down the slopes, a hasty search, pockets filled with sherds and then the final thrill of mental and physical satisfaction ! There was no illusion ; it was a vast camp enclosure for chariots, and it was of Canaanitish date. All conditions of the problem, topographical, literary and archæological were satisfied : it must be Hazor ! Subsequent study of the materials confirmed the impression, which has long ago been accepted by all students. By noon the " expedition " equipped for a three-day tour was back upon the shores of the Sea of Galilee. That was a lucky hit, but the process whether long or short illustrates the way to localize a site.

Having now answered the first part of our original inquiry, we may turn to the second, how to set about the actual digging.

Excavation is not a happy-go-lucky affair ; it has become a science, and as such calls for careful organization. The actual numbers taking part will of course vary, but each expedition must include a director, a staff of helpers, and the native workmen.

When conditions involve the clearing of much sand and debris, as was the case at Meroë in the Sudan, 500 men could be controlled by three trained helpers. Where delicate work is involved, as in the clearing of a tomb or a house-floor, the task is best done by a few really skilled diggers. But on most occasions about twenty workpeople can be supervised by each experienced student.

At Jericho many grades of native labour were employed, including Bedouin and Druses, men, young women, and boys. They were arranged for purposes of supervision in three or four groups, each under the control of a young, though adequately experienced, archæologist, and their wages ranged from 12 to 6 piastres a day (2s. 6d. to 1s. 6d.). Following up the digging were a number of "experts", as we called them, selected for their skill and aptitude, who cleared and removed all fragile objects, the find-spots being marked with red labels by the local supervisor as the work proceeded. Such valuable help was rewarded with double pay.

The material equipment, also, has to be thought out beforehand, and may include anything from a bodkin to a crowbar. It would be little short of disastrous, when overhead expenses are necessarily heavy, to be held up for a split-pin or a packet of films. Local transport of the necessary gear and supplies may also present problems, especially if camels are the only means available. In the removal of debris light railways and tip trucks are freely used; at Meroë, where the limits of the ancient city could not be predetermined, being covered with a forest of prickly acacias which had to be cleared as the work advanced, we devised a system of light tip buckets running on overhead wires so as to clear the intervening obstacles.

On an undisturbed site the excavator's task can be pursued methodically ; for knowing how mounds grow, he may reasonably expect to find a succession of " floors of occupation ", separated by " layers of destruction ". The surface debris would be carried away, then limited areas of the ruined city would be cleared layer by layer, thus exposing the important features of each period. The earth and rubbish from each room is removed with a small trowel or a special tool, and the objects found are put into a basket, labelled, and then carried back to headquarters. The supervisor also keeps a careful note of the exact place from which each basketful has been taken, and if any object of special interest is discovered, he marks the position and level upon his chart.

Watchfulness can never be relaxed. Objects which may seem trivial at the time may assume great importance in the light of further investigation ; and for this reason the systematic recording is supplemented by the work of a photographer. This important member of the " dig " takes pictures of the actual progress of the excavation as well as of objects and buildings as they are uncovered. An architect or trained draughtsman also makes scale plans and sketches of architectural features, and either he or an artist draws with accuracy any pots or potsherds that may be of interest. Last year our records included 2,000 sketches made in the field by different members of the staff, and 250 finished drawings.

This finished work is, of course, done at headquarters, where indeed other tasks are constantly in hand. The day's discoveries must be carefully noted and filed, negatives must be numbered and stored, photographs registered and classified, the journal and accounts made up for the day: for the morrow brings fresh duties.

Another branch of work claims special mention: this is the cleaning and preserving of the more fragile objects found, processes which involve simple apparatus but careful preparation. One needs for this a wooden bench, with brushes, acids, dishes, an electric battery, paraffin wax and a spirit lamp.

Hot wax is a great stand-by. A fragile fragment may be coated with it, even together with the surrounding earth; and when all is cool it can be safely moved and handled. Sometimes in Egypt the shell or surface of a wooden object may be apparently intact, but the inside reduced to powder by that mischievous pest the White Ant: the simple expedient of soaking it thoroughly in melted wax will usually save the specimen. Strengthened provisionally in this way, objects can then safely reach an expert or museum for final treatment, and it is easy to melt out the wax.

Many concoctions in tubes and bottles for sticking broken bits together will be found on the repair bench. The actual mending is a slow process. If we are dealing with a pottery vessel, the fragments have first to be selected and washed, then fitted together like a picture puzzle. But this work is tedious ; for an hour one makes good progress, then nothing more seems to fit, until someone comes in fresh and with a superior grin says, " Why don't you try this piece with that one ? " No matter how, day by day little bits are fitted ; then these in turn come together and the pot begins to grow. There may be ten or twenty pots growing on the bench together, propped up in sand, or against boxes, or in the corners of shelves, until at last they are handed over, not perhaps perfect but sufficiently complete for others to draw and photograph.

Though most members of the staff have their special jobs, they do not work all the time in watertight compartments. In practice some of the tasks are shared, and everyone has a fair share of supervising some part of the actual digging.

This brief outline of our organization would not be complete without some mention of the place in which we eat and sleep. We do not live in tents if it can be helped. That sounds attractive and picturesque, but in practice is not at all satisfactory, especially in windy places. There is nothing in experience to beat an empty house, the bigger the better. At Jericho, after various experiments, we were lucky enough to find two conveniently placed native houses in which we set up our camp furniture. There we lived comfortably for the last three seasons. As drawing office we secured a well-lit room overlooking the mound, and in the empty stables below were stored the Arabs' tools.

Such work is not only interesting to us, but usually means a great deal to the local people, who readily adapt their lives to our requirements. The scene at sunset is picturesque : men, women and boys all flock to the well to wash and then move away in little groups, some towards the village singing as they go, others towards caves in the hills where they make their temporary homes.

What now of Jericho itself? How did we find it and what did it look like at our first visit? No search was necessary in this case ; the Biblical and other literary indications all pointed to the west side of the lower Jordan not far from the fords. There is a modern village of much the same name, and every villager knew the ancient site a mile farther towards the hills, where a captured spring bears the name of Elisha's Fountain, given to it in the Middle Ages. There could be no doubt about its identity, for there is no other site of the required antiquity in that part of the Rift, and this one is not only traditional but it satisfies all the references in the Bible and other sources. There, just on the edge of the cultivable area, rose the long irregular mound, half dug or washed away, full of deep holes and trenches—a sorry spectacle for an archæologist.

The excavation of this city proved indeed particularly complex. The position of its defensive walls varied with different epochs, extending at one time to the foot of the mound, and at others only encircling the brink of the slope ; so that at certain levels some parts of the mound lay outside the protected area. Irregularities in the ground added to the difficulty of interpretation ; for important buildings might be raised on a natural or artificial hillock above the contemporary dwellings and streets. Problems of this kind are, however, fairly normal. The chief complication arose from the effects of former excavations, which, owing to a technical difficulty in the disposal of debris arising from the lie of the ground, had covered many spaces that had still to be examined, and on the other hand filled up numerous excavated buildings with debris since consolidated by time and rain. The merit of the work itself is not in question, but its effects created pitfalls like these at numerous points.

Clearly the conditions for further excavation were difficult and demanded special caution, so we devoted our first two seasons to trial investigations, in order to locate the leading features of the city, and to relate them to the different defensive walls. Part of our task was to ascertain which portions of ground remained unexplored, and even the debris had to be sifted, in most cases with disappointing results. There was, however, one spot at the foot of the northern slope covered with a great heap of earth which was shown as a blank in the former excavator's map ; so in the third season we set to work to shift the whole pile of 2,000 tons ; and we were rewarded by finding a great stone revetment, on top of which was a parapet, and against this some houses of a later occupation.[1] In front of this rampart ran a deep dry fosse, a defensive feature quite unexpected ; and we were able to trace the piling up of an artificial filling which had enabled attackers at a certain time to assault the parapet and apparently capture the city.[2]

Another piece of investigation made in the course of our preliminary trials was the cutting of a deep section from outside the city right up the slopes, linking all the defensive systems of different periods. As yet we were without any fixed points, groping in the dark, not knowing much about the local styles of pottery or other objects. Such a trench, besides showing us the relations of the various walls and ramparts, was calculated to teach us the characteristics of each Age, and so provide definite leads which might be applied to all further investigations. This cutting, which was fifty yards long and was carried down to the prehistoric levels, proved very helpful, though in solving some problems it introduced several fresh ones. We had as close supervisors of this work a trained architect and an engineer-surveyor, under whom a record of the precise find-spot of every important object or series of potsherds was registered by its actual height above water level. From these records,

[1] See Fig. 2 and Pl. XIIa. [2] cf. II Samuel xx, 15.

amplified by subsequent discoveries,[1] it has now been possible to prepare a revised diagram (Fig. 2): it shows at a glance the relation of the various wall-systems to one another and to the general development of the mound.

The value of such trenches will be apparent.

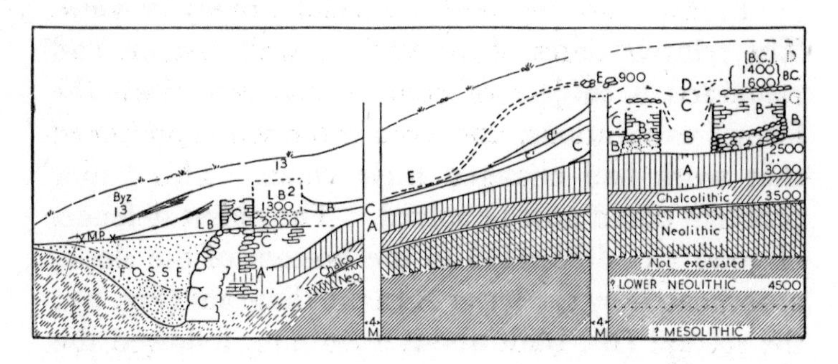

FIG. 2.

Diagrammatic section through the northern slope.

They are a master-key to the solution of difficult questions and a sure basis for further investigation, as they present to the excavator a view of the successive " layers of occupation ", serving for him much the same purpose that a chronological outline does for the historian. Some excavators of a more modern school think that trenches are wasteful; but since in our view they save from damage much more than they destroy by defining the " lie of the land ", and many important details can only be appreciated by this method, we adhere to our golden

[1] The terminology also has changed since the original diagram was published: thus the culture called then M.B.A. i (i.e. Middle Bronze Age, 1st phase) now becomes E.B.A. iii (Early Bronze Age, 3rd phase), and so on.

rule : " When in doubt or difficulty, cut a section ". Needless to say each such trench will be proportioned to the problem : a foot deep and three feet long may be enough ; it does not need to assume the importance of the one we have described.

In this case we had a special object in view. The relative dates of the various wall systems had remained a subject of controversy ever since the former excavations, and even those who conducted that work had changed their views. This major problem could now be solved. The oldest defences of 3000 B.C. descended to the bottom of the slope, as indicated by the letter A in the diagram (Fig. 2) ; the second (B), built about 2500 B.C., followed the brink of the slope probably as a dual system. The third (C) surrounded the foot of the mound with a giant stone glacis, constructed about 1800 B.C., while the fourth (D) returned to the brink, and ran along the top of the second system. The traces of this were not well preserved in the section just described, but its position has been established, as may be seen from the photograph and drawing on Plates XVII and XVIII.

With the destruction of this fourth system about 1400 B.C. the old city of the Bronze Age was brought to its end. But in the diagram there may be noticed the higher slope of a lime revetment ending in traces of stonework ; this was all that remained in this area of the city as restored about 900 B.C. in the time of Ahab. Connecting these systems in the diagram are lines representing

PLATE V

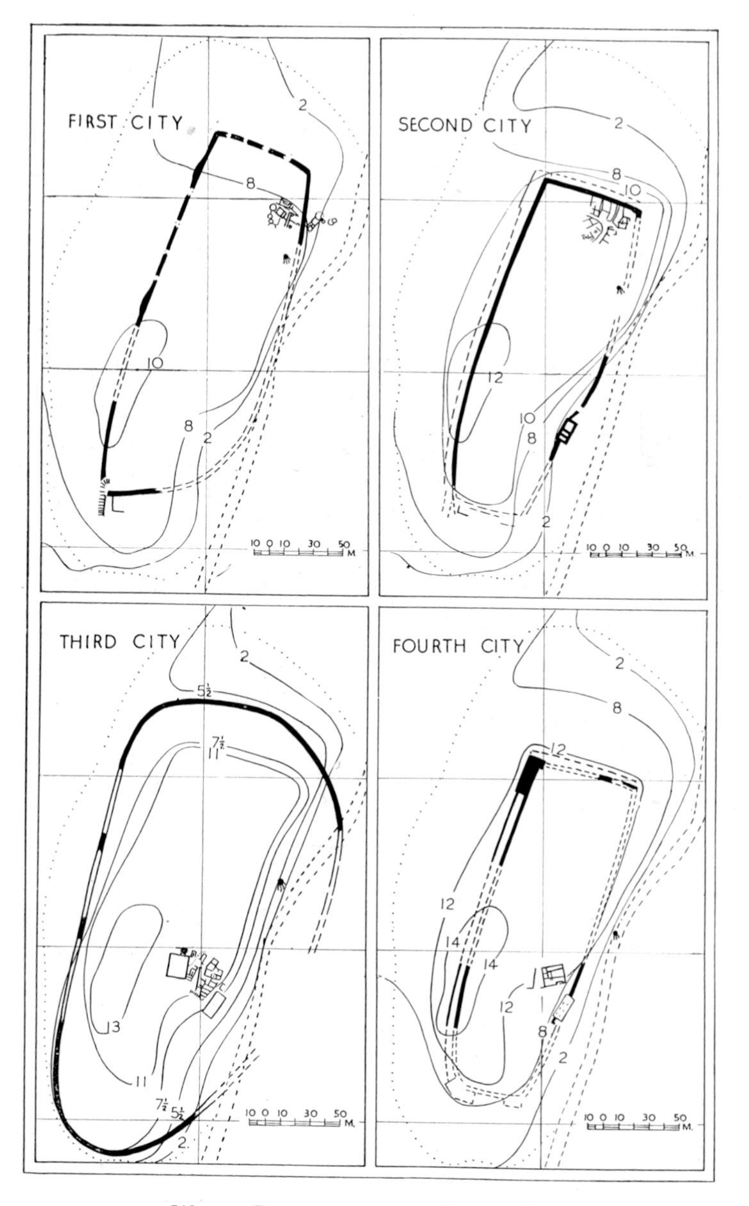

WALL PLANS OF THE FOUR CITIES

PLATE VI

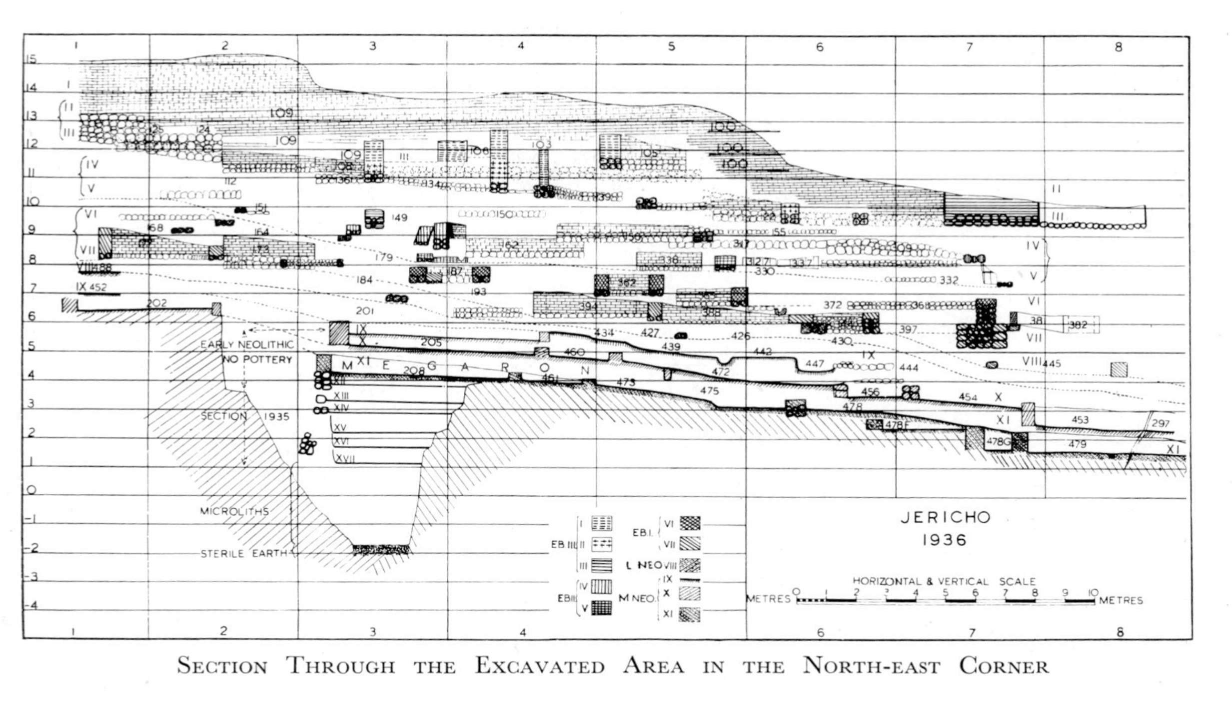

SECTION THROUGH THE EXCAVATED AREA IN THE NORTH-EAST CORNER

successive ages of occupation. Further details of the deeper levels are shown by a separate section, based on wider excavation in the north-east corner, reproduced on Pl. VI ; while the links with higher levels in the Palace area are indicated in similar fashion in Fig. 3.

Each Age is represented by a distinctive culture, defined by objects made or imported, particularly

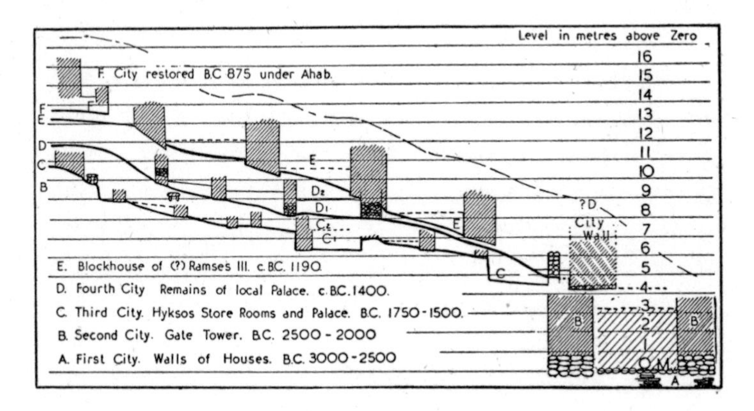

FIG. 3.
Layers of Occupation on the slope of Spring Hill.

tools and weapons, trinkets, and domestic utensils. In the earliest Ages tools and weapons were made of flint, later (about 3000 B.C.) of copper, later still of bronze ; these materials have in fact lent their names to the periods in which they were chiefly used. Within each period such products remained essentially the same in character, though varying maybe from generation to generation in some detail as a result of experiments or improvements in technique. By far the greatest stand-by of the excavator is the pottery, and this for two reasons : it is almost imperishable, even though smashed to pieces, and more than any other product of man's hands it reflects his tastes, the fashions of the age, his home industries, and maybe his trade relations. Illustrations of this may perhaps be found in our own dining room : the local crockery on the table ; the Dresden china in the corner cupboard ; Chinese vases on the mantelpiece ; the teacups perhaps from France.

In the East, and in most places under old-world conditions, where floors and pathways were largely mud, broken pottery lay about, the big pieces thrown out of doors, the rest inside, where they got trampled into the ground and so remain to tell their story to the excavator of to-day. The study of pottery, including potsherds, has for these reasons become a special feature of modern archæology ; for each period had its peculiarities. The earliest pots were usually built by hand, next the slow wheel or *tournette* was devised to assist in regularity of shape, then the quick wheel upon which pots are "thrown" to-day. Some periods specialized in form, others in decoration. Naturally the common pottery of simple folk, such as the cooking pots, had less tendency to change, particularly in its fabric, which contained special ingredients for resisting heat. But looking at each Age as a whole we can find plenty of ways of distinguishing one from another. Some objects, particularly imported specimens, may resemble dated examples from other sites or areas, and so provide chronological landmarks, which give a date not only to the objects but to the layer in which they were found.

So much for the theory, but in practice at Jericho it was not easy to apply. In addition to the local disturbances ancient and modern, we found that the pottery taken from the deep cutting described above, of which we washed and examined 150,000 fragments, was largely unfamiliar, much of it indeed was quite new to archæology. This enhanced the interest of the work but did not give the clues we so much required, though we did ascertain which were the older and which the later styles, and manage to distinguish in broad outline the successive "levels".

It had become obvious that we must secure better information about the local arts, especially the pottery styles, before we could solve the problems of a site so much disturbed as this. Accordingly we decided to look for the burying place, for a necropolis is usually well stocked with pottery; but for some time this escaped us, though our search parties scoured the bare ground in all directions as far as the hills, and the Air Force helped us by taking bird's-eye pictures. At last, almost in desperation, we lined up a hundred workmen in two rows three miles apart and made them work slowly over all the intervening ground. On the tenth day a man came running into our headquarters with a couple of potsherds and reported that others were coming to light. Dashing off to the spot we arrived just in time, for the band of workers was converging upon an area where whole pots were coming to view, and picks were swinging with all the vigour of misplaced enthusiasm. When the excitement had been curbed and the army of labourers marched elsewhere, the tombs were located one by one just below the stony surface, where their presence had never been suspected, and fortunately they proved to be largely undisturbed. The site was actually only about 250 yards to the west of the city, and one of our photographs on the mound shows it in the foreground (Pl. IIa). The larger tombs were scooped out under the gravel, with a small opening leading to a chamber and a stone to close the entrance; but most of them were round open graves.

The full excavation of the necropolis took two whole seasons, and even in the third year a few more tombs were found as a result of continuous search; but in the end the area seems to have been exhausted. The results were, for us, momentous: not only had we secured direct evidence reflecting the local burial customs and pottery styles of Jericho, but we had established contacts with Babylonian and Egyptian art and chronology. This gave us just those materials required for the full and final interpretation of our discoveries within the city.

After the preliminary explorations on the mound had shown us the lie of the land, and the clearing of the tombs had provided the necessary clues, we settled down to the systematic excavation of two areas within the city which seemed most likely to give fruitful and reliable results. The one,

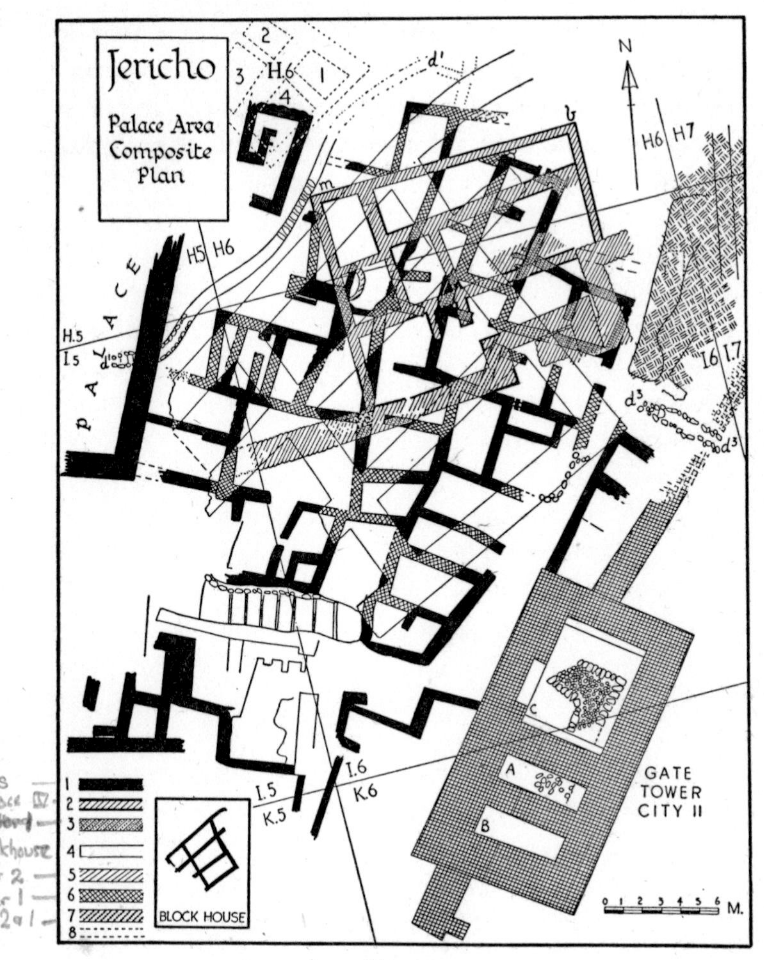

FIG. 4.
The succession of buildings in the Palace Area.

on a small hill overlooking the spring, proved to be the site of the royal palaces in successive ages. The other, in the north-east corner of the walled enclosure, plunged us at once into the earliest period of the city's history, and led us down to unsuspected depths 50 feet below the point of attack. Here we uncovered the vestiges of one of the oldest settlements of man yet known, perhaps indeed the oldest in the world.

CHAPTER III

THE EARLIEST SETTLEMENTS

Late Stone Age : 4500(?)–3000 B.C.

CHAPTER III

IN the last chapter we told how we found unexpectedly the remains of Late Stone Age buildings deep below the foundations of the Walled City in the north-east corner of our area. These Neolithic deposits, for such they proved to be, led us down stage by stage to a further depth of 23 feet, a fact which in itself suggests a very long period of occupation and development. Where these early settlers came from remains a mystery; but it would seem that under the conditions of unchallenged isolation which the Jordan Valley enjoyed at that time, there was little to disturb the peaceful habits of their lives. So far as we know, they found no need to protect their settlement with enclosing walls, but lived there securely generation after generation for more than a thousand years. Throughout this long period, though there is evidence, as we shall see, of marked stages in their cultural progress, there is no sign of any radical change in the essential character of the settlement. Houses were built and rebuilt in proximity to one another, primitive religion took shape, and domestic life became established; so that as early as 4500 B.C. the inhabitants of the site of historic Jericho had already formed themselves into an organized society.

We must, however, recall the fact that these Neolithic remains are not the oldest traces of settlement here, though our knowledge of the original occupation is very limited. The earliest remains were found 64 feet below the Bronze Age walls of 3000 B.C., and at that depth our excavations had become little more than a sounding in which wider investigation was impossible; so that we really do not know anything about the mode of life of the original settlers, and can only make conjectures from the primitive and generally pigmy character of their flint implements. Though seemingly characteristic of the Middle Stone Age or Mesolithic Period, these are thought by some experts to be related possibly in some way to the developed Neolithic culture which overlay them. This comment seems justified by the fact that man of the Mesolithic Period elsewhere used caves or shelters of which we have hitherto found no actual trace at Jericho. The problem of the original settlement thus remains unsolved, though the traces certainly exist, forming a deposit 6 feet thick upon a sterile bed of marl.

In this connexion an observation made during the progress of this investigation, simple though it seemed at the time, now claims a moment of consideration, as it may throw light upon the problem. The earth at these depths was wet: we use the word designedly to express something more than dampness, such as might be expected. The section of the cutting reproduced on Pl. VI will show that the bottom of this hole was well below the present ground level outside the mound, and must have nearly reached the water table. But as the spring was said to be fed by a subterranean rock channel connected with other supplies at the foot of the mountains we did not at the time ascribe the excess of moisture to that source. More recently we have, however, seen a photograph of the spring as it appeared in the eighties of last century. Unfortunately it is too damaged for publication; but it shows the waters of Jericho issuing from a rock and cascading in a stony bed at a point which was further to the north-west and higher than the basin which now marks their outlet. A diviner actually traced a buried stream in that direction, following it across the modern road and into the area which we were excavating. In the light of the photograph it seems probable that he really sensed a line of flow, now covered over, from the original spring further up the channel. The first inhabitants may thus have dwelt in rock shelters or small caves by the open stream which subsequently became blocked and covered by the debris of occupation. As the ages passed, efforts would be constantly made to retain the spring within the immediate circuit or just outside the limits of the settlement; and when at last the village became a "city" surrounded with walls provision would be made for protecting this vital source and securing ready access to it for the village needs. But the process being continuous the exit of the waters is now fully a hundred yards from its original position, and further movement has been arrested by building large pools which the water enters at numerous points.

Even before the Neolithic settlement a part of the original channel seems already to have become covered, as the earliest floors of occupation within the excavated area were based upon a wet deposit, the traces of which rose through successive floor levels to a height of 12 or 15 feet. This may explain to some extent why the earlier buildings are found to have been frequently rebuilt, and a special technique developed for preserving the walls and floors. It is true that mud bricks, such as were used throughout the life history of Jericho, were peculiarly liable to decay. As the mud of which they were made was lacking in cohesive properties, it was commonly mixed, even at this early period, with straw and chaff. But this medium was liable to be devoured by small insects, and this process would tend rather to accelerate than restrain the normal disintegration of such bricks arising from exposure to drying heat and occasional strong winds. Sometimes too, in winter, rain falls very heavily, so that unless the outer walls were protected from the elements, they would be liable to perish. To these common causes of decay there should be added the effect of earthquakes, visibly traceable at certain of these levels where great fissures appear through walls and floors. These were, however, exceptional, and their traces are generally quite marked. In the absence of any special signs of burning and destruction, we must attribute the frequent rebuilding of houses to the normal processes of decay aggravated by the underlying damp. Experiment and experience taught the inhabitants how to combat these defects and the methods they devised lend character to the architecture of this period.

The floors of houses were laid upon a bed of limestone chippings, about two or three inches deep, the finer pieces towards the top, which the action of moisture tended to weld into a hard mass. Both walls and floors were finished also with a smooth lime surface, which was freely coloured with bold splodges of red or brown, and then burnished by frequent rubbing with a suitable smooth stone. To judge from the condition of the upper series of buildings, these finished surfaces were frequently re-burnished, and rubbing stones tinted with pigments were amongst the few objects found upon the floors. It is noteworthy also that some of the passages and pathways around and between the houses were finished in the same way, from which it would appear that whole areas of buildings were covered with a common or continuous roof. A farm-yard and building of to-day, in full view of the site, are actually covered in this way; and the roofing materials, comprising rough timber, reeds and mud, remain much the same as those used by the Neolithic settlers.

The most interesting of these early houses to be discovered at Jericho had its original foundations in the very lowest Neolithic layer, the date of which must remain uncertain, but was probably not later than 5000 B.C. It was found to have been reconstructed upon its original lines, and its floor level raised, no less than six times ; all the seven superimposed floors were found intact, having survived the periodic destruction of the walls. Its chief room, which measured 15 by 18 feet, was much larger than the average houses of later ages ; and, consequently, its roof timbers would need

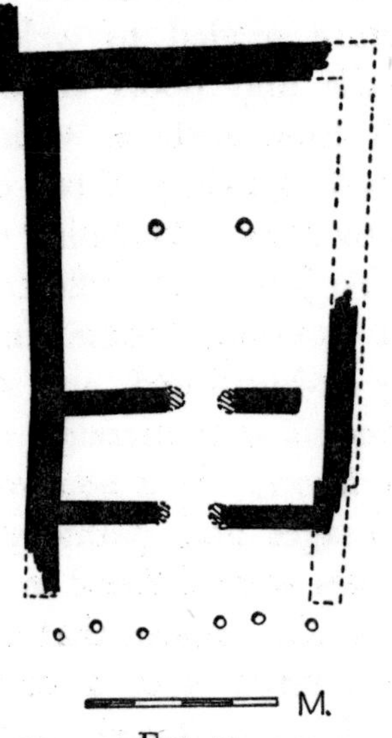

FIG. 5.
Plan of Stone Age Shrine

support in the centre. In the topmost and third floors post-holes were actually discovered in good preservation and still plastered round the base where the wooden post once stood.

The best example of advanced architecture, probably a temple, was found towards the top of this series. It was fronted by a portico of six wooden posts, which gave access to a wide antechamber ; and from this a doorway flanked by engaged columns (made of curved bricks) led to a large inner chamber. A special interest is attached to its discovery in that this design bears a close resemblance in plan to the developed *megaron* of ancient Greece, though more than 2,000 years earlier in date.

From Homer we learn that in the home of Odysseus, which was probably typical of the average chieftain's house, the *megaron* was the principal room, where meals were cooked and eaten, and host and guests met in social intercourse. It was approached through a door set in the portico of the entrance-court, and immediately beyond it lay the women's apartments. There was a hearth in the middle, and pillars between the two main doors supported the roof. The chief difference between the Homeric *megaron* and that of Jericho lies in the fact that the latter contains no central hearth ; but this was probably because of the climate. Instead of a hearth was found the socket of a post to hold up the roof.

This building was one of those reconstructed upon the same plan age after age : the three top levels were examined in detail, and lower down such walls as could be traced followed always the same lines, making use of the earlier foundations. Evidently this was a time-honoured building of special character and design. Outside its chief entrance were found numerous votive figurines of clay and mud representing chiefly domestic animals, such as cows, goats, sheep, pigs and dogs, as well as certain emblems of fertility. Such animals and other figurines have been found elsewhere in similar contexts, as for example in the excavations conducted by Dr. Speiser at Tepe Gawra and at Billa, and by Mr. Mallowan at Brak, in Mesopotamia, where however they belong to a much later age. In the foreground were a number of tiny rooms with trap openings, which look like sheep pens. It may be readily inferred that this building was in fact a temple, and its associations indicate a pastoral cult. We probably do not err in supposing that the original Neolithic settlers who domesticated animals and introduced agriculture were devotees of the Moon God, the shepherd's friend. Sheep pens are actually mentioned in connexion with the cult in a Babylonian hymn to the Moon-god Shîn from which these lines are quoted :[1]

> Oh Shîn, watchman of the temple thou hast been made
> . . . , guardian angel of the temple
> Thou hast gathered the oxen, bringest back the sheep
> . . . .
> To the ewes and lambs thou (givest)
> Sheep of the pens therein thou . . .
> God of the new light art thou ; . . .
> To the leading goats (?) the kids thou (givest)
> With the kids and she-goats the oxen (thou makest to lie down) together
> God of the new light art thou ; . . .
> . . . cows and oxen among the sheep (thou pasturest ?)

That pastoral people of this part of the world

[1] As translated by the late Professor Langdon, in *Babylonian Liturgies*, p. 1.

PLATE VII

NEOLITHIC FLOORS AND MODEL SHRINE

PLATE VIII

VOTIVE FIGURINES OF ANIMALS: AND NEOLITHIC FLINT IMPLEMENTS

should worship the Moon, especially under conditions of climate like that of Jericho, was natural. Where herbage is scanty for most of the year and shade is rare, the Sun is too fierce to be regarded as their friend; on the contrary in desert regions he brings drought and thirst. But the Moon is beneficent and kindly, dispelling the terrors of darkness, while bringing coolness and rest to man and beast.

The recognition of this building as a temple may help also to explain the facts behind two remarkable interments discovered near its site. One was that of a man who had obviously died a violent death; his neck seemed to have been broken by twisting his head round; and his body was held down, as it were, by a fairly large stone. Possibly he had been caught in the act of violating the sanctuary, or stealing temple offerings: it is at any rate fairly clear that he was punished for some crime. In the other case a man's head was found to have been completely severed from his body, as may be seen in our photograph on Plate IXb; but as the excavation continued we noticed a continuous fissure across the floor of the room and running up the walls, telling of an earthquake which by a remarkable coincidence had subsequently produced this curious illusion of decapitation.

Another burial discovered in the excavation of these buildings was that of a child, found between the floors. There is, however, no evidence of sacrifice: the burial of small children below the floors of houses is a primitive custom not by any means confined to Palestine. The idea of the spirit of the young child hovering about the home brings consolation to bereaved parents. In this case burial within the sacred precincts possibly implied in a particular sense the idea of the communion with the God and the pious hope of an ultimate reward or blessing.

Domestic life seems to have been well established at Jericho from the beginning; and this conclusion is borne out alike by the arrangement of the houses and by the domestic character of various objects found in them, such as mortars, pounders and grinders, as well as burnishing stones (some of which, as stated, were very smooth and bore traces of brown or red pigment), bone points, sea shells, stone rings, pieces of coloured stone and pumice, a few beads and some perforated shells.

Flint working, for the making of tools and weapons, claimed necessarily first place among the industries of this Neolithic community; and though remaining throughout uniform in technique and method, it almost attained its zenith as a craft. To secure the specimens, many of which are very small, we employed sieves, handled by women in pairs, sitting in oriental fashion as they worked. The result was gratifying; for whereas in the first season, when we sieved only the earth from selected areas, we obtained eleven hundred specimens, in the second, sieving all the earth with adequate organization, we secured more than ten thousand. These were all examined by an expert on the spot. They comprise a full range of Neolithic implements of a special Palestinian kind, including nearly 150 arrow-heads (mostly with wings well defined and strong tangs), more than 800 sickle blades, as well as numerous scrapers, borers, gravers, blades of all kinds, and other varieties of useful tools. Many of these were very small, resembling in some ways the pigmy specimens of the Microlithic deposits at the bottom of the cutting. The material used was a fine-grained nodular flint, brown-grey in colour. It is perhaps significant that so large a proportion of the worked flints represent tools rather than weapons. Arrow-heads were doubtless made and used for hunting and so liable to be lost, but only one javelin-head appears in the list though, one would think, this class of object would be preserved if only for protection against wild animals, while purely defensive weapons were relatively few. On the other hand, nearly all the fabricated tools were evidently designed for domestic, pastoral and agricultural purposes—sheep shearing and skinning, the sewing of skins for clothing, ploughing, reaping, winnowing and so on. It seems as though warfare was so little known as to call for no special weapons or organization. Truly this was in those days the "Land of God"; and it was so named by the Egyptians from earliest times.

A great stage in cultural progress was marked by the invention of pottery. We use the word "invention" deliberately, because under the isolated conditions of the time and place this was hardly a case of learning the art from neighbours and travellers, much less of adapting the characteristics of other people's pottery to local needs and circumstances. Indeed the evidence of experimental invention at Jericho is fairly clear. The moulding of clay figurines in both human and animal shapes has already been mentioned in connexion with the temple of the Moon-god, and apparently these are by far the earliest known examples of plastic art, at any rate in Palestine. They were followed by more ambitious attempts, by no means unsuccessful, to model the human form itself. These and other experiments, described below, immediately preceded the great invention for which they had prepared the way.

In the earliest stage, pottery made its timid appearance as a basin scooped in the earth and lined with a coat of marl or limey earth about 1½ inches thick. A development saw the borders of the vessels carried up above the floor and sometimes assuming the dimensions of a large bin, the base of which was always below floor level. This marly material, however, was non-cohesive ; it contained as yet no binding material like chopped straw and but little clay. Nor was it baked, so that when pinched now after exposure to the air it falls into fine powder. For this reason very few if any complete specimens have survived, but the rudimentary character of this ware is illustrated by hundreds of fragments.

The beginnings of pottery making were indeed primitive, but the art soon developed as experiment proved the advantage of using clay. Next it was found that the mixing of chopped straw or fibre with the clay gave greater cohesion to the fabric, so that vessels after drying in the sun could be moved and used for carrying. Thus the first pots were made. One can imagine with what excitement the community would follow the

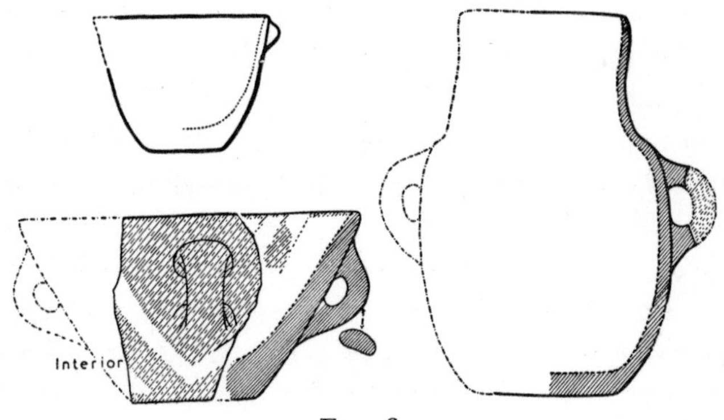

FIG. 6.
The Earliest Pottery c. 3700 B.C.

progress of this discovery ; with what zeal the craftsmen or craftswomen and their children would vie with one another in experiments of form and fabric. Shapes long remained simple, however, though knob-like handles were devised to help in carrying or for suspension. It was accident no doubt that showed the hardening effect of fire, after which the laborious efforts to secure a water-tight surface by pigments and burnishing were rewarded with more rapid progress. With the first initial difficulties overcome, the first pot-makers were able to make further experiments in shapes, and even (as our illustrations show) to apply their pigments to trace lined devices upon their more finished products. This phase, however, was not reached without a long progress of experimentation, of which happily some unique examples were sufficiently preserved for us to secure a record.

The most remarkable object of the primitive class was shaped somewhat like a bee-hive, 40 inches high and 30 inches wide. Its base was 6 inches deep, and its walls 1½ inches thick. It seems to have been the model of a building, possibly a house or an elaborate kind of grain bin. At ground level it had a pavement of stone slabs, and a dummy doorway blocked by a stone which rolled in a built-up frame. A little higher was a recess with solid walls and floor. At two-thirds of its height the model was crossed horizontally by a floor supported by a central pillar, and the domed roof was supported in turn by a similar feature. On either side of the top floor were small "windows", about 2½ inches in diameter, piercing the thickness of the walls. Unfortunately this object fell to pieces during the process of conservation, but not before a series of photographs and a measured drawing had secured a record of its unique character. One of the photographs is reproduced on Pl. VIIb.

As in the case of the *megaron*-like temple of the Moon-god, the interest of this discovery is enhanced

PLATE IX

THE EARLIEST POTTERY: AND EARTHQUAKE EFFECTS

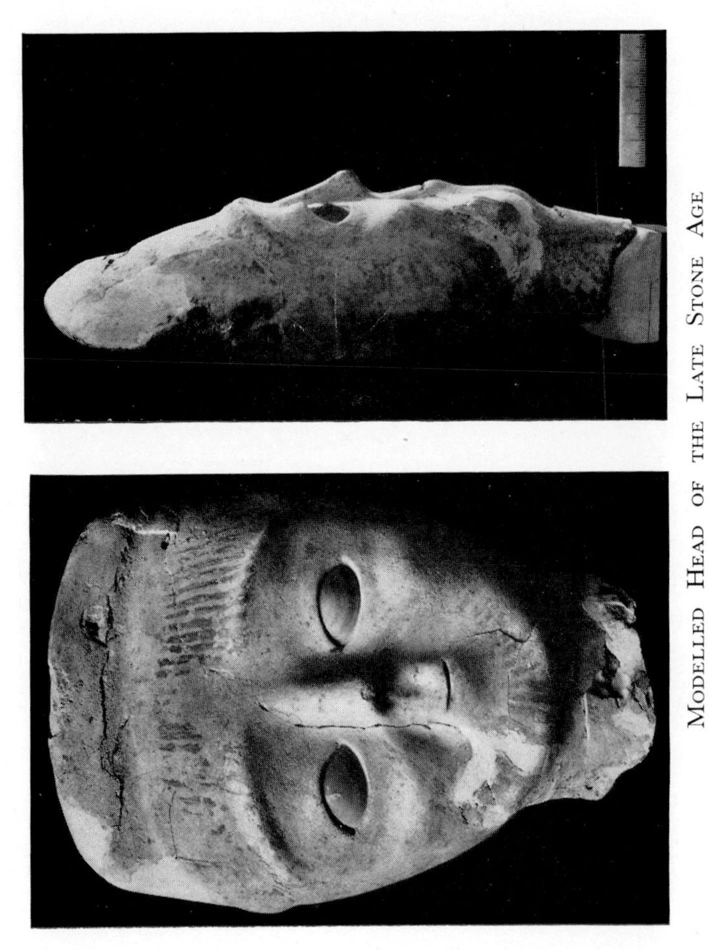

Modelled Head of the Late Stone Age

by its resemblance to certain early Greek shrines, notably the Argive Heræum: both possess an upper storey, twin columns and other common features, and it is thus possible that the Jericho model represents a shrine.

More amazing as examples of plastic art are some images or statues also discovered at this stage in the excavation. They were found in two groups, and though the bodies were very fragmentary, in each case a man, woman and child seem to form the theme. From restoration skilfully effected by the Palestine Museum in Jerusalem, it appears that the male figure in each case was much taller than the others, in fact nearly full height, the woman was half that size, while the infant was no larger than a doll. The limbs of the larger figures show considerable sense of movement, and in general the modelling is by no means crude, muscles and other details being worked out with a certain freedom and without undue exaggeration. The clay surface is carefully smoothed and treated with a drab or reddish pigment. In the better group the clay is unbaked, though no doubt sun-dried. It was therefore a matter for congratulation to find, when the head was finally lifted, that the face was well preserved. The hair and beard are represented by reddish-brown radiating lines, and the eyes are fashioned of selected sea-shells, which were presumably inserted from behind, as the clay which represents the eyelids shows no signs of any joins.

The other group, which was generally similar, and included a small foot with modelled toes, rested upon a hearth of loose stones and so was partly baked, but whether placed there intentionally for that purpose is not certain. It was found inside a small ante-room of a house. This was exceptionally well preserved, and comprised a larger room 18 feet long and 12 feet wide, with an ante-chamber, possibly the bedroom, separated by a wall and a raised sill, and in the corner a grain bin. The main wall was wavy on the inside, following the contour of its foundation stones, and the doorway led out between this wall and the small room beyond, in which were the fire-stones and statues.

As usual at this period, both walls and floors were covered with plaster, carefully smoothed, finished with red colouring, and burnished. The burnishing stones were found, and they were greatly worn and smoothed with use. The bed of small stones upon which the floors rested was mixed with lime, which was apparently unslaked, but contained a small proportion of earth and other ingredients. The surface, presumably from wetting the lime with the paint and from constant polishing, had formed a coherent crust, varying from one to two inches in thickness. This was an interesting corner of our deeper excavations, for it was at the back of this house, just one floor higher, that were discovered the best examples of the hole-in-the-floor pots that could not be removed.

LAST PHASE OF THE STONE AGE

The last phase of the Stone Age at Jericho well illustrates the continued isolation of our site. Whereas other parts of the ancient world, from Babylon to Egypt, had begun to experiment with the use of metal and entered upon a "Chalcolithic Age" (as explained in our first chapter), the people of Jericho remained practically unaffected by this innovation. This does not mean that this period saw no development or change in the civilization of Jericho; on the contrary it marked a distinct phase with its own pottery, flint industry and architecture. The fact that no trace of metal was found is therefore all the more remarkable, especially as the way lay open for outside contact through the channels already described. Jericho was affected by the spirit of change, but retained throughout this Chalcolithic period its individual Neolithic culture, modified and enriched in various ways, but aloof from the direct influence of the outside world.

This distinctive character is readily illustrated by the development of its pottery, which differs from that of the underlying Neolithic phase, being more developed in form, variety and technique. The admixture also of flint grit and sand with the clay gave greater cohesion to the fabric. Vessels were now sometimes rotated on a mat in their making, and this new device facilitated better finish and evolution of form. Handles were strap-like and firmly welded to the body of the vessels with a broad attachment. The surface was sometimes burnished, but usually hand-smoothed before baking. Colour when applied was mostly drab with the decoration in large bands of purple or brown : some finer wares also made their appearance, and these were covered with a slip decorated with linear devices. Generally

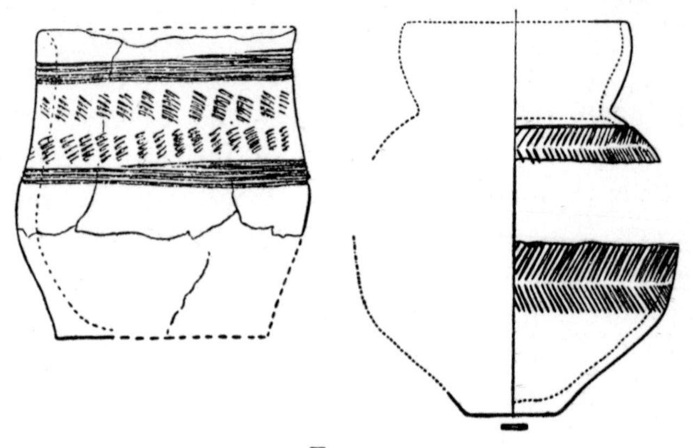

FIG. 7.
Late Neolithic Pottery : c. 3300 B.C.

speaking the art of painting pottery seems to have deteriorated, and to have been less practised than in the previous period, while decoration by moulded and incised motifs tended to develop. One fragment bearing the design of broken and waving grass or corn stalks is not only pleasing from a decorative standpoint, but discloses power of drawing and observation ; and linear motifs executed by incision, both upon pottery and a number of stone bowls, became a standard feature.

It would seem, from various discoveries illustrating this concluding phase of the Neolithic

Period, that the people were becoming more agricultural ; and this suggestion is borne out by an analysis of their flint implements. These included, indeed, a large curving implement, a splendid specimen, which seems to have been designed specially as a sickle—a marked improvement on the primitive tool hitherto used for reaping in which a number of small blades were hafted like a row of sharp teeth upon a stick.

In general the flint industry—as was the case with the pottery—shows a marked modification when compared with the underlying specimens. This is to be seen in the smaller size of the arrow-heads and certain technical differences of many of the sickle blades, and in other ways. An analysis of 2,400 worked flints shows that sickle blades (used for cutting corn and threshing) were in great preponderance over all other finished products, numbering 243 ; other objects used in agricultural or pastoral life include 50 scrapers, 7 end scrapers, 10 core scrapers, 1 celt, 4 chisels, 1 pick, 4 knives of "tabular" flint, 33 gravers and 54 borers. On the other hand, arrow-heads were not only small but numbered only 37.

As previously noted when discussing the earlier deposits, the relatively low number of arrow-heads cannot, however, be taken as a true indication of the proportion of arrow-heads in use, whether for hunting or other offensive purposes, because they would be used almost exclusively outside the city where they might be lost, whereas most of the other implements mentioned would be used within the walls.

The evidence afforded by the flint industry of increasing agricultural requirements is corroborated by the architecture of the period. One of the most striking features of the houses we excavated was the number of pits sunk through the floor levels and clearly designed for the storage of grain. The house walls were normally of mud brick, or mud slabs upon foundations of stone ; and occasionally the lower part of the building would be further strengthened on the outside by a series of standing (" orthostatic ") stone slabs. These would not add much strength to the structure, but would prevent the too rapid decay of the lower courses exposed to rain or water standing in the narrow streets. Otherwise we know very little of the architectural details, as most of the area was found to have been disturbed by the new-comers of the Bronze Age.

This last phase of the Late Stone Age was thus a period with special characteristics, and curiously unaffected by the contemporary civilization elsewhere ; no single object found at Jericho could be said to have its origin in the far North or East. It is true that the pottery shared features in common with specimens from Ras Shamra and from a site near Gaza, and, as these places are relatively far removed from one another, it is not unreasonable to infer that such parallelism may have extended at any rate through Syria. This is borne out to some extent by the complete identity in numerous details of form and style between the pottery fragments of Jericho and Beisan, which stood, as we have seen, upon the valley-road linking Jericho with the Syrian coast. Another settlement at Ghassoul, opposite to Jericho across the Jordan, bears witness also to the diffusion of common elements in this Age ; but the differences in this case are marked, and almost suggest different stages of development, unless they are to be explained by a lack of effective contact between the two sides of the Jordan.

A definite and welcome link with the outside world appears at the very close of this Chalcolithic Period. On top of the deposits of this Age were found two objects of Egyptian origin, a stone palette and a mace-head of alabaster, both characteristic of a late pre-dynastic phase in Egyptian art, rather earlier than the establishment of the First Dynasty. This discovery not only indicates the opening up of contact between the Jordan and the Nile, but enables us to ascribe the close of the Chalcolithic Period (the last Neolithic phase) at Jericho to the end of the fourth millennium, rather before 3000 B.C. With this round date begins the history of the City.

The Stone Age at Jericho.

Third Neolithic Period. *c. 3000-3500 B.C.*	Contemporary with the later Chalcolithic cultures of Mesopotamia (Tell Ubaid and Jemdet Nasr Periods). New styles of pottery; developed flint industry.

Second Neolithic Period. *c. 3500-4000 B.C.*	Probably contemporary with the early (Halafian) period of the Mesopotamian Chalcolithic cultures. Possible relations with Tepe Gawra. Invention of pottery: plastic figures: continuous flint industry. Developed architecture. Shrine of the Moon God.
First Neolithic Period. *Before 4000-c. 4500 B.C.*	Evolution slow: local flint industry stylized: origins of architecture: no pottery. Community life.
Mesolithic Period. *Before 5000 B.C.*	Microlithic flints: possible rock shelters; suggestions unconfirmed.

CHAPTER IV

JERICHO BECOMES A CITY

Early Bronze Age : 3000–2000 B.C.

F

CHAPTER IV

ALTHOUGH the site of Jericho had been occupied by man from a remote period in the Stone Age, no walls seem to have been built around the settlement for the protection of its inhabitants until about 3000 B.C. This development not only marked an epoch in the history of Jericho but was symbolic of a changing world.

For hundreds of years the Neolithic inhabitants had enjoyed the tranquillity of their isolation, but danger began to loom ahead when the expansion and activities of distant societies resulted in repeated movements of peoples from their settlements in search of new homes beyond their borders. The chief driving power for these migrations seems to have originated in Southern Babylonia, where the grouping and fusion of important cities, consequent upon the discovery that harder weapons could be made by mixing tin with copper, had gradually established the domination of that district over an ever increasing area along the Tigris and the Euphrates.

This inevitably led to fresh colonization and a displacement of weaker peoples westwards, along the lines of least resistance; so that before the end of the fourth millennium the culture of Mesopotamia and of Babylonia had begun to take root in Syria. The foundations were thus laid for the building of the first Babylonian Empire ; and by 2500 B.C. the great Sargon of Accad extended his conquests to the Western Sea.

The intermittent pressure from these movements was felt in Palestine : the once boundless horizon of Jericho was gradually narrowed down, and before the end of the Chalcolithic period other settlements were already established as near as Beisan in the Jordan Valley and at Ghassoul just across the river.

Meanwhile the process of fusion had been at work in the Nile valley, and about this time Egypt also became united under its first dynastic ruler. Though no written records have been found at Jericho itself, the fact that the chronological outlines are known from this time in the two great centres of civilization, Babylonia and Egypt, and that cultural links are established between them and Jericho, makes it possible to look upon subsequent developments of our site as illustrations of the general course of history. In short, we may regard the Prehistoric Period as having ended, and the history of Jericho as beginning, with this dated epoch.

In Palestine many great Canaanite cities have been shown by archæological discoveries to date their origins from these times, such as Hazor, Ta'anak and Megiddo on the north-eastern trade route, and Shechem, Beeroth and Jerusalem in the hill country to the south ; and probably the same is true of most of the great cities of the plains.

The new world now enfolded Jericho, where also a complete change of civilization, coupled with the signs of destruction of the previous settlement, argues a change of race. The general increase of population throughout the country involved a division of lands between the different city groups as well as protection for their flocks, and this led rapidly to the construction of defensive walls.

THE FIRST CITY. Presumably the people who now occupied the country were already familiar with walled cities and the organization of urban life. There is proof at Jericho that this new population brought with it radical features of Babylonian civilization; and there can be little doubt but that the new city was founded and fortified by a people migrating either from further north in response to pressure from beyond, or from Mesopotamia itself.

The main wall of the First City seems to have followed generally the outlines of the earlier Neolithic settlement, and enclosed an area of four or five acres towards the northern end of the site, within which was the spring. Being deeply buried beneath the debris and masonry of subsequent occupations, it has only been traced at intervals. On the western side it seems to have followed a low defensive scarp, and towards the north to have descended nearly to the bottom of the slope, where it turned eastward and returned again in a line more or less parallel with the western wall at a distance of about 100 yards. The further line of the eastern wall remains uncertain : in enclosing the spring it seems to have swung outwards, as some houses of the period were found below the present road near the southern end, whence it may have connected by a curve with a visible return at the corresponding end of the western wall, as shown in outline on Pl. V. The length of the city from north to south, so far as we can tell, was about 250 yards ; thus in shape while fairly regular it was long and narrow. To judge by such of the original buildings as we have examined, it was laid out with houses or rooms along the city walls, separated by a narrow street four or five feet wide from a double row of houses in the middle. No gateway of this period has been found, but there seems to have been access near the south-west corner by means of steps which presumably rose above the rampart at that point.

The main walls were constructed of large slab-bricks of mud, and the masonry is further distinguished by a thick bonding of bituminous earth, dark in colour and almost as thick as the bricks themselves. This method of building is peculiar to this age and it enables us to recognize also the house-walls of the period. It is also a Babylonian feature.

Some buildings of this period were located early in our explorations of the site near the present position of the spring, south of the later gate-tower to be seen in the plans (Pl. V) ; but for more precise information we devoted two whole seasons to the systematic excavation, layer by layer, of an area in the north-east of the walled enclosure. This work disclosed seven successive levels of occupation belonging to this Age, four of them actually of the First City. On the bottom-most of these, forming part of the original plan of

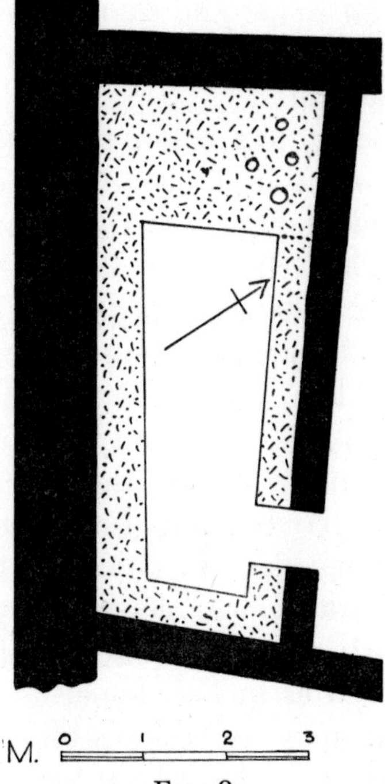

FIG. 8.
Plan of Babylonian Shrine.

the city, was found a small shrine. This was of Babylonian character, having a relatively large dais at one end and a continuous "mastaba"-seat built against the walls. Dais, walls, seats, floor and doorway were all carefully plastered;

and the precincts of this shrine were separated from the other buildings uncovered in this layer by a stouter wall than usual. In the vicinity, and belonging to this level, were found several related objects, notably a small libation altar and also a remarkable piece of stone, long and relatively thin, of natural shape and smooth with the patina of time, presumably a " Mazzebah ", a central symbol of the cult.

In this corner, just below the bottom floors of this period, was found one of the chronological links with ancient Egypt, in the shape of a mace-head of a style well known in that country just before the first dynasty began. This piece of evidence, corroborated by the presence of a similar mace-head and a stone palette just above the Chalcolithic level in another spot, not only established the round date for the inception of the walled city of Jericho, but shows that the movement now taking place in Palestine, the establishment of city states, was generally speaking contemporary with the development of dynastic rule in Egypt as well as in Babylonia.

Though it may be reasonably inferred that the new-comers must have been better armed than their predecessors, unfortunately this cannot be confirmed, as no weapons of this period were discovered, unless we include various decadent flint implements. In advanced centres elsewhere the Bronze Age had begun, but there is no sign that the knowledge of alloying copper with tin was shared by these new inhabitants of Jericho.

On the contrary, what is called the Early Bronze Age of Palestine was in practice at Jericho (and indeed in other places) an entirely copper-using period ; during which even flint implements were still used for ordinary domestic and agricultural purposes. This fact, like the use of stone long after copper was known (see p. 59), illustrates a pronounced cultural " lag ", covering indeed a whole era in each instance, due to the early immunity and isolation of the site. Better communications and increased contacts now began rapidly to close the gap ; while the primitive elements surviving in the life of the inhabitants began to disappear.

The flint tools and weapons of the Early Bronze Age no longer attained anything like the fine standard of the Neolithic Period : they are known as Canaanean. Out of the four hundred specimens examined by an expert, only one, an arrowhead, proved to be of an offensive character, and that of course might have been destined for hunting. Long knife-like blades, some of them also thick and strong, are indeed characteristic of this period, but they were presumably designed for domestic uses. Sickle blades for reaping and threshing were again the most numerous category, while large fan-shaped scrapers and other specially shaped tools may have been used for preparing skins. Other industries are represented by gravers, borers and a small number of tiny specimens for finer work.

Agriculture now evidently became an established

and successful industry, and the earliest architectural features of the site confirm this impression. Numerous large silos or grain bins were found at the earliest level, some passing through into the debris of the earlier occupation, others actually resting upon the preserved floors of the Chalcolithic period which served as a convenient foundation. The art of laying and burnishing the floors, so conspicuous during the previous Age, was lost ; for even though some of the old floors were utilized where they happened to be preserved, the next series of buildings shows only indifferent pavements of potsherds or stones, or more frequently of beaten earth.

In plan also these earliest houses were adapted to the life of a pastoral and agricultural society. At first they were relatively big, for they comprised a courtyard, usually with baking oven, a storage bin for grain, and an open space presumably for sheep or goats, as well as one or two small living rooms down one side. The size of these earlier buildings must have necessitated central pillars to support their expanse of roof, but no trace was found of any masoned post-holes.

In construction mud bricks were used upon a laid foundation of coarse undressed stone. The bricks were oblong and not baked. Walls were frequently curved or round to conform with the necessities of planning within a circumscribed area ; but though large round rooms were constructed these were probably not used as dwellings. They rather marked a great development of the

PLATE XI

Architectural Features of City I (3000-2500 b.c.)

PLATE XII

Glacis of City III. and Ramparts of Cities II and IV

system of storing grain ; the great number of these bins and their strength suggests that the cultivation of cereals in the locality rapidly became a successful industry. Among the produce actually found there can be recognized grains of millet, barley and lentils ; and there is a suggestion that almonds also were already used for food.

While examining the contents of one store vessel on the spot (for it was too fragile to move), we noted that it contained the seeds and skins of grapes, and mixed with these were small fragments of cloth. These were quite clear when first viewed, and we were able to count the number of warps and woofs, eleven and twelve respectively ; but after a short exposure the least puff of wind would destroy all such traces if measures were not taken to protect them. Happily we were able to secure some specimens between thin sheets of glass, and they are preserved in the Liverpool Museum.

The community obviously prospered and became rich in grain and animals ; and as their own numbers increased the housing accommodation, restrained from lateral expansion by the city walls, became a serious problem. So busy were the people with their flocks and herds and the irrigation of their corn fields that the finer arts and crafts seem to have remained at a standstill. The population seems to have enjoyed long periods of peace : for in the earlier part of this period such rebuilding as was noticed seems to have been due to normal replacements and not to general destruction. Under such circumstances life by the Jordan

Valley would tend, as in all epochs, to become stereotyped and uneventful. But perhaps weaving and the making of wine (as suggested by the fragments of cloth and grape-skins found in the same vessel) may have been introduced by the new-comers ; while dregs of barley coating the bottom of big vessels suggest that a sort of beer was already being made. Pounding-stones for bruising meat and flat grindstones for crushing

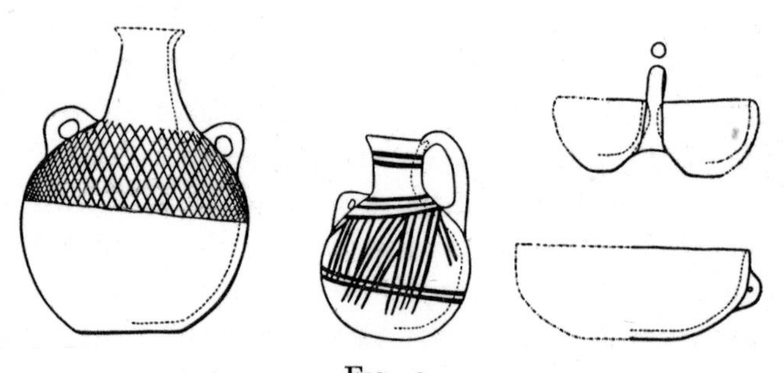

FIG. 9.
Early Bronze Age Pottery of City I : c. 2800 B.C.

corn indicate the staple foodstuffs of the day ; but other material for the picture of these times is wanting.

The art of pottery-making was highly developed from the start, and the finished product gives proof of a greatly improved technique when compared with the primitive methods of the earlier epochs, with which it has no relation. The processes of refining and mixing the clay were better understood ; while the freer use of the hand-wheel by the potters, for making open-mouthed vessels and finishing the necks of jugs, led to greater symmetry of form. Though many vessels were left plain, quite a number were decorated with painted linear devices, of which the favourite theme is a series of multiple lines, sometimes arranged chevron-wise, and sometimes interlacing. The pottery was largely utilitarian, comprising open bowls and dishes, storage vessels with broad handles, as well as two-handled jugs, small and large, for holding fluids. The baking of pottery was now a matter of routine, and with the problem of watertight vessels thus solved, elaborate burnishing of surface, characteristic of the earlier periods, was no longer common. Cooking seems to have been done in wide, flat vessels, but as yet it would seem that no special fabric had been designed to resist the heat of the fire. The bottoms of vessels were mostly flat at this time ; while the primitive lug-handle, so-called from the suggestion of a pierced ear, was still used on small vessels, apparently for suspension. The " ledge " handle, wavy or indented in design, was however more characteristic of the Age, and it appears on most standing jars, large or small.

The interest of the community in their herds, and evidence that the original Babylonian influence was maintained, is seen in a remarkable piece of carving belonging to the middle of this long period. This is a small head of a bull executed in ivory, now darkened as by accidental firing. It was evidently imported. Not only is the execution Babylonian in style and technique, but the animal represented has been recognized by an expert as a

Babylonian breed.[1] The object was found low down in some detached rooms near the present position of the spring, and with it were some vases of special style, the date of which may be estimated at about 2600 B.C. The presence of this object fills a gap in our story : it suggests that throughout all this early period Jericho, and hence presumably other cities of Palestine, remained within the sphere of influence of the established Babylonian dynasties.

THE SECOND CITY (2500-2000 B.C.). During the thousand years represented by this Early Bronze Age culture, about the time when Babylonian influences became widespread under the first Dynasty of Accad (c. 2500 B.C.), a Second City was built, this time distinguished by a notable development of military architecture. The old walls here and there show signs of burning, and upon the ruins the new city was remodelled in its entirety. The date suggests some connexion with world movements spreading from Babylonia, rather than a purely local cause, such as destruction due to an earthquake, which might necessitate rebuilding on a large scale, but would not account for the marked elaboration of the new ramparts and other features.

The new boundaries were moved slightly southward, and on the west they extended beyond the old line which they followed, but the northern slope was no longer enclosed (cf. Pl. V). The defensive walls were conceived on a noble scale,

[1] From a report communicated to the authors by Sir George Adam Smith.

ten feet in thickness, compactly built of firm square bricks, yellow in colour. The main wall as disclosed by our excavation still stands in many places, a magnificent witness to the art and ingenuity of this period of revival. At the same time the "town-planning" at the north end had to be modified, partly on account of the withdrawal of the north wall to the brink of the slope, which thus interrupted the two lanes of communication already mentioned. These were now joined by a curving cross-lane which communicated with a new system of houses against the inside of the new north wall. Another factor was the obvious increase of population, which led to the dividing up or elimination of courtyards, and to a reduction in the size of dwellings. There is actual evidence that the expansion, as the population increased, was upwards, as is to be seen on a grand scale under similar restrictions of floor space in New York City to-day. A party-wall between two rooms in the north-east corner was found to stand nearly sixteen feet high, indicating an original two or three-storied building, and this in its turn was later capped by a room with a sloping roof.

Possibly it was at this time that an outer screen wall, later to become much in evidence, was originally planned, to protect the more vulnerable places in the defensive lines. It was thinner than the main wall and its foundations were found a little way down the slope at a distance of about four yards.

The finest architectural monument of Jericho

was conceived also at this period. This was a gate-tower opposite the present position of the spring. It stood upon a solid foundation three feet deep, formed of rough stones laid in four courses. It had a length of about sixty feet, a width of thirty feet, and still rises in places above its foundations to a height of thirteen feet: the topmost portion, however, showed traces of reconstruction which added somewhat to its height at a later stage. It was built of grey brick, set with remarkably regular bond and true face.

This tower contained three deep vaults or chambers, which no doubt originally formed storerooms or dungeons of a kind, for only one of them had signs of any entrance and that not at the bottom. Their contents on excavation did not help to clarify the question of their original purpose. They seem to have been gradually filled up during the subsequent centuries, but at the bottom were found potsherds distinctive of the period of their origin. Later on this tower became a conspicuous feature in the development of the area, surviving from age to age; but at the first doubtless it served the double rôle of defending the city gate immediately to the north and protecting the water supply, which by this time had already approached nearer to the position in which it is now found. It is noticeable that the line of the city wall abutting against the northern face of this tower bent outwards, as though to enclose the spring; and, by connecting this bend theoretically with the north-east corner of the city wall found in our excavations, we are able to restore the whole outline. Elsewhere the enclosing walls were more or less straight except at the south end, where the new sector of walling followed a curving contour. Notwithstanding these changes, the area enclosed remained much the same, being rather less than five acres.

The inception of this great undertaking was contemporary with the introduction of new styles in pottery, which supplement but do not radically

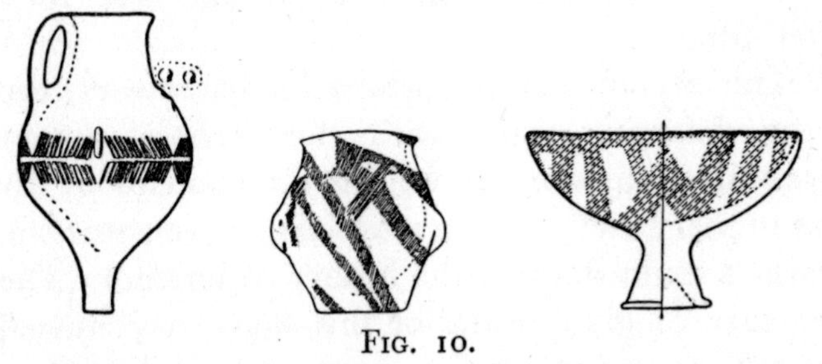

FIG. 10.
Early Bronze Age Pottery of City II : c. 2300 B.C.

change the main features of the ceramic arts of the Early Bronze Age. Our investigations were greatly helped at this stage by the discovery of a contemporary tomb, as described in Chapter II. This burial place, which we call "Tomb A", had originally been a large cave or grotto, the roof of which had collapsed, covering its instructive contents; so that though many of these were broken, those in the lower levels or placed under ledges were complete; while numerous pottery vessels (which constituted the bulk of the tomb furniture) could be restored. Altogether we took out some 800 vases, as well as a number of trinkets, amulets, flutes of bone and other small objects illustrating the arts and customs of the period. This large burial place had apparently a communal character, and was presumably that of a tribe or family living within the city. It seems to have remained in use for two hundred years or more, the number of burials amounting to perhaps five hundred ; and as the grotto became filled and more space was required for fresh interments, the ancient remains within were brushed on one side time after time.

This Second City, of which the gate-tower, the great defensive walls with three contemporary levels of occupation, as well as the contents of the communal grave, are the most instructive witnesses, marks a main stage in the history of Jericho. The necessity of giant walls of this kind may indeed suggest a period of increased unrest, but they certainly bear witness to the improved powers of the inhabitants to meet such an emergency. For three successive building periods, covering as many centuries, the city had no further set-backs, and one can only picture normal life resumed, coupled with the warning of increasing menace from outside.

CHAPTER V

JERICHO A HYKSOS STRONGHOLD

Middle Bronze Age: 1900–1600 B.C.

CHAPTER V

ABOUT 2000 B.C., or rather later, a major catastrophe overwhelmed the great old City which had endured and preserved its early culture for a full thousand years. It is disappointing not to be able to assign a definite date or cause to an event of so great a magnitude. It does not seem on this occasion to have been brought about by earthquake, which figures strongly in our story at other epochs, but rather by some political upheaval. This is indeed fairly clear, because the site lay more or less derelict thereafter for some time, perhaps a century, and when finally the city revived it is found to have been entirely replanned and reconstructed upon fresh lines, with a new and improved defensive system ; while an entirely new culture, that of the Middle Bronze Age, replaced the old. Moreover the change was general, and it affected in similar fashion all the great cities on the highlands above the Jordan valley, Jericho's nearest surviving neighbours ; while many early settlements in and near the southern end of the Rift never revived at all.

Looking beyond the immediate horizon of Jericho, we find this change to have occurred more or less at the time when exceptionally powerful dynasties were established in Egypt and in Babylon.

More nearly, as recent discoveries have shown, an influential vassal of the Babylonian kings had become firmly seated at Mari, on the nearest bend of the Euphrates. There thousands of inscribed tablets have been discovered, and their decipherment, it may be expected, will in due time throw a new and welcome light upon the development of the situation which provoked this widespread change of race and culture. Meanwhile the Biblical narrative of military activities in the Book of Genesis which describes the war of the " four kings against five " gives perhaps the most reliable indication as to the course of local issues in which old Jericho and its neighbours became submerged.

> " *And it came to pass in the days of Amraphel king of Shinar* [Babylonia], *Arioch king of Ellasar* [Larsa in Babylonia], *Chedorlaomer king of Elam, and Tidal*[1] *king of Goiim* [nations]*; that they made war with Bera king of Sodom, and with Birsha king of Gomorrah, Shinab king of Admah, and Shemeber king of Zeboiim, and the king of Bela* (*the same is Zoar*). *All these joined together in the vale of Siddim* (*the same is the Salt Sea*). *Twelve years they served Chedorlaomer, and in the thirteenth year they rebelled.*" (Genesis xiv, 1.)

Chedorlaomer appears to have been the leader of this confederacy ; and the supremacy of Elam over all that region of Western Asia about the time of Hammurabi is attested by ancient documents. If, as was long supposed, " Amraphel "

[1] Tidal simulates the Hittite name Tudḫalia with the ḫ dropped, as was frequent.

can be accepted as the Hebrew reproduction of the name " Hammurabi ", and modern chronology is right in assigning the latter's rule in Babylonia to a time near 2000 B.C., then this war must have concerned Jericho very closely. In any case, it was in the district of the " five kings " who rebelled against the " four ", and must have felt the full blast of this incursion.

One significant fact emerges from our excavations. The materials bearing upon the history of the site in the first phase of the new era, though fragmentary and inconclusive, none the less constitute a culture-level which spread over most of the ruined city. These traces of occupation, to quote from our formal report[1] at this time, " indicate the incoming of a people without " resources or aptitude for building. Their short " period of settlement is unlike all other epochs, " in that it is marked by no fresh fortifications or " architectural development. It may well repre- " sent the vanguard of an Aramæan migration, a " conjecture which seems to accord with the " northern or Mesopotamian relations of their " peculiar ceramic wares." Technically the affinities of this new pottery, " with its flat bottoms and lug handles ", are found in the preceding rather than the subsequent period.[2]

The suggestion of this last observation is that the new-comers were not altogether strangers to the established Babylonian influence, but different

[1] *Liverpool Annals of Archæology* XXIII, " Jericho City and Necropolis," Sixth and Concluding Season, 1936 : p. 74.
[2] ibid., XXII, p. 156.

from those who subsequently took possession of the site.

"*And Lot lifted up his eyes and beheld all the Plain of Jordan, that it was well watered everywhere, before the Lord destroyed Sodom and Gomorrah, like the garden of the Lord, like the land of Egypt, as thou goest unto Zoar. So Lot chose him all the Plain of Jordan; and Lot journeyed East . . . and dwelled in the cities of the Plain, and moved his tent as far as Sodom.*" (Genesis xiii, 10-12.)

The statement that Lot, though a nomad chieftain, resided with his family in Sodom is not inconsistent with the possibility that detachments of his tribe made their centre upon the site of Jericho. Even to-day the heads of nomad tribes which have secured the grazing rights in the partial deserts east of the Transjordanian ploughlands commonly dwell themselves in town centres, such as Amman (the ancient Rabbath-Amon) and Kerak (Kir of Moab); while their tribesmen, in family groups under the general direction of clan leaders, roam far and wide on organized circuits, eking out in this way the scanty pasturage round the occasional water holes to sustain their flocks and herds. At the time of Lot's sojourn in the Jordan valley some relatively important towns like Sodom and Gomorrah still stood at the south end of the Dead Sea, and doubtless certain restrictions would be placed in their vicinity upon the movement of Lot's herdsmen. But so far as we know the rift valley to the north of the Salt Sea, with Jericho in ruins, was unpopulated ; and this deserted site with its perennial spring and green oasis would inevitably attract nomadic groups, to whom it must have been indeed " a haven of contentment ".

THE THIRD CITY. How long this state of affairs endured it is not possible to say with any

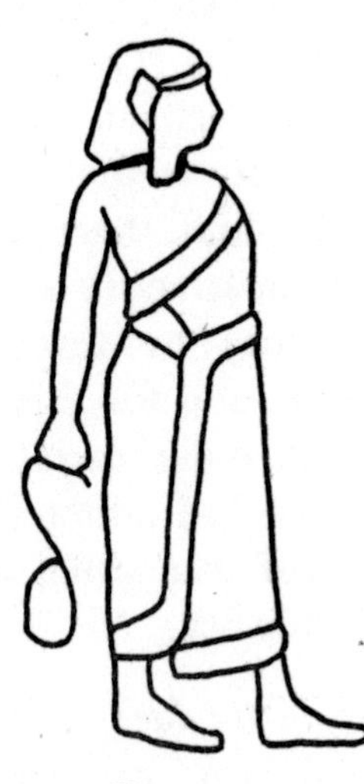

FIG. 11.
Canaanite Costume : from a Scarab.

certainty : maybe two or three generations. Then came a further change in race and civilization. This time material traces are plentiful : new walls were built and the City came again into being. The new epoch is called the Middle Bronze Age ; and its culture though progressive remained radically the same for about 400 years, from about 1900 till 1500 B.C., notwithstanding great political changes involved in the Hyksos domination (c. 1750 B.C.) and the Egyptian conquest a hundred and fifty years later. In this case, as we shall see, the culture actually outlived the city as now planned.

The new-comers were the Canaanites: descendants according to the Book of Genesis of the tribe of Ham, and hence more nearly related to the Egyptians than to the Hebrew Semites (the stock of Lot and Abraham). Though we have little knowledge of the movement of the Canaanites which established them as the leading element in the population of the land, there can be little doubt but that they came in strength and took possession of the old town sites by force. Possibly they introduced the horse, and for this reason preferred the plains, confining older racial elements to the hills. Certainly they had adopted both horse and chariot as an arm of war when first seen by the light of Egyptian history.

> "*Amalek dwelleth in the land of the South; and the Hittite and the Jebusite and the Amorite dwell in the mountains; and the Canaanite dwelleth by the sea and along by the side of Jordan.*"

This passage from the Book of Numbers (xiii, 29) is found to convey in four lines an admirable impression of the new ethnographical distribution. The Amalekites were desert peoples around the south end of the Jordan Rift; the Hittites were now established in north Syria and Asia Minor, and frequently involved in raids and warfare in the south, leaving settlers even as far as Jerusalem and

Hebron. The Jebusites were a particular clan, of mixed Hittite and Amorite stock, said to have peopled Jerusalem; while the Amorites, better known further north, seem also to have preferred the hill country, and according to Israelite tradition had established a powerful kingdom, that of Og, in Bashan beyond the Jordan. To the Canaanites fell the cities of the plains, including Jericho in the Jordan Rift.

Our excavations on the site, while not uncovering any extensive buildings of the early phases of the Canaanite settlement, have shown clearly that the newly established culture was that of other Canaanite cities, and that it passed through similar stages of development. The new rampart also, on being laid bare, proved to conform with the system adopted generally in the strong places of the country. Its principal defensive feature was a great stone glaçis, 21 feet high, sloping inwards as it rose, which entirely enclosed the enlarged area of the city. This was twice as big as previously, for the new line followed the foot of the now considerable mound, leaving the old walls still partly visible as an inner line around the brink of the slope.

While the whole conception of this new rampart was majestic, its construction was equally imposing. Solidly built of large, rough-hewn stones, laid and set with surprising regularity, it was provided with special features for defensive purposes. All around, about half way up its slope, a "string course" of stone projected slightly, in order to cause a missile launched from above to bound outwards against the attackers. This feature may be seen in our photograph on Pl. XIIa. Nearer the bottom, again, where the size of the building stones was proportionately larger, one course in particular was constructed of enormous blocks each more than a ton in weight. This girdle was clearly designed to resist the battering-ram.

These lower courses of the glaçis descended, moreover, beneath the ground-level of the day, and the trench thus formed was widened out into the proportions of a fosse which apparently surrounded the whole area on the side where the ground stood high. On top of the glaçis, again, was constructed a parapet of brickwork, about five feet high, with a " firing step " against it on the inside.

This formidable and elaborate defensive system, when complete, comprising glaçis, parapet, and outer fosse, not only illustrates a great development of military architecture, but indicates also the resources and organization of the new community. We found no means of telling how long the building of this rampart in its completed state had taken ; but indeed, to judge by comparison with other sites like Shechem and Jerusalem, it probably evolved by stages, and we may suspect that it was not perfected until the coming of the Hyksos. We only know of one other case of a stone glaçis surrounded by an outer fosse, and this is a gigantic rampart completely encircling the mound of Tell Keisan, possibly the Biblical Achshaph, in the plain of Acre, uncovered by the Neilson Expedition in

1936. Here also we may suspect Hyksos organization, for the site came within the direct sphere of the Canaanite centre at Hazor. Here the vast camp enclosure of Hyksos origin which abuts upon the Canaanite city is enclosed by ramparts of beaten earth, 60 feet in height, and these are in turn encircled by a deep outer fosse. The latter feature, then, would seem to have been a peculiarly Hyksos elaboration.

The Hyksos appeared in Canaan about 1750 B.C. or just before. Who they were or whence they came is by no means certain. They seem to have been almost welcomed by the Canaanites; and in any case their introduction of the chariot as an arm of war, and their obvious capacity for military organization, would have borne down any disunited resistance. Reinforced it would seem by Canaanite allegiance, they overran lower Egypt, where they remained in effective control for five generations.

It was during this period that Jericho, under the Hyksos regime, attained its greatest extension and the height of its prosperity. The protected area was now about nine acres, which was nearly the size of contemporary Jerusalem. The ramparts already described were now complete, and they enclosed within their circuit the entire water supply. Inside, the ancient mound, now considerably raised in height by the accumulated ruins of previous ages, became again the scene of active life and industry, and the community evidently prospered. The single fact that hundreds of splendid vases, many of them in perfect condition and well dated by no less than 165 scarabs of the Hyksos period, were recovered from widely separated private tombs of the necropolis shows that this prosperity was general.

In the heart of the City, on a peak of ground overlooking the spring, rose a royal palace, the most elaborate dwelling uncovered upon the site. The main block, which was square, crowned the highest part of the knoll, and it was surrounded at ground-floor level by a sort of roofed ambulatory, in which would be half-cellar store-rooms, offices, stables, etc., much as in the arcaded basements of many houses of the East to-day. Of special interest are the traces of a stone-lined drainage system[1] connecting with a W.C., a novel feature which finds contemporary parallels in Babylonia. The slopes on either side, and particularly towards the East, were honeycombed with store-rooms,[2] arranged in rows, stacked full of storage vessels sealed in numerous instances with the signet of a Hyksos ruler. The very proportions and solidarity of the palace building show that the ruler of Jericho at this period had attained both wealth and power; and the contents of the extensive store-rooms committed to his care seem to explain the source of his increased prestige.

It has been mentioned that the Hyksos warriors used Canaan as a stepping-off place for their invasion of Egypt, and that Hazor was one of their military headquarters. Jericho was evidently an

[1] d^1 and d^3 in Fig. 4. [2] I in Fig. 4.

advanced base connected with that movement and particularly concerned with the commissariat. Though of no special strategic importance, it was a safe place for a supply depôt, owing to its isolated position ; and though off the beaten track, good routes connected it with the main lines of communication. There was a further advantage in its situation, in that it controlled the direct line of approach to the rich cornlands beyond the Jordan.

FIG. 12.
Scarab of the Vezir's Scribe.

In garnering these the standing of Jericho's king would obviously be useful ; so, from the absence of any trace of struggle, we may believe that his offer of allegiance was accepted peacefully as an arrangement of mutual advantage. He became in fact the chief of an important unit in the Hyksos organization. Associated with him as guardian of the Hyksos stores or " treasury " was a resident official, whose title " Scribe of the Vezir " appears upon scarab-signets and jar-sealings recovered from the store-rooms ; the names of two persons who held this office were *Senb. ef* and *Se. Ankh*, both characteristic of this period.

Our excavations have shown that the Palace

of this period and its store-rooms not only covered the whole slope overlooking the spring but extended as far as the gate-tower and the old wall of the Second City ; and indeed a few rooms were eventually built over and upon this wall, which still rose high above the ground around the spring.

The photograph on Pl. XVIb gives a good idea of these store-rooms as they appeared during the excavations. Most of them were found to be stacked with grain-bins containing charred remains of barley, oats, millet and sesame, as well as a special kind of sealed jar which still retained traces of wine and barley-beer. In quite a number of instances these store-jars, which were about three feet high, had been buried with their mouths at floor level. This would seem to have been done as a precaution ; for in a climate like that of Jericho, where in summer everything is dry and brittle, the danger of fire and even of spontaneous combustion of the grain and other stores was very real, and the burying of vessels in this way would help to limit the zone of any such outbreak. Several instances were observed where the contents of a few jars or a whole room had actually been burnt, and in one case the flames had swept through the doorway of an adjoining chamber. In all, some sixty-eight store-rooms were examined and their contents noted ; and though some varied in the nature of the containing vessels and the provisions stored, evidently all formed part of a vast repository, far surpassing the resources and requirements of a mere local ruler.

The shapes and sizes of the vessels were mostly proportioned to the nature and bulk of the provisions to be stored ; but not all were of a purely utilitarian character. One group of chambers in particular contained a number of smaller vases of special quality, high finish, and elegant shape, characteristic of the age (Pl. XIIIb). It would seem to have housed the temple offerings and furniture. Included among the contents was a

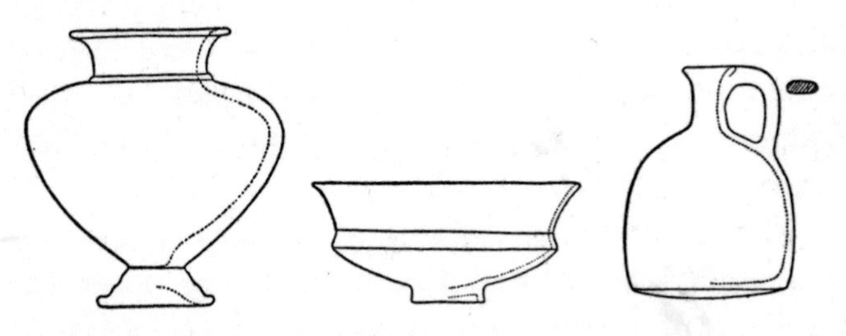

FIG. 13.
Middle Bronze Age Pottery of City III : c. 1700 B.C.

tall chalice, decorated with a circuit of painted triangles and meanders, the whole finished with a red surface which was highly burnished. A handle attached to the shoulder reached high and finished with a downward curve upon the rim. Up the middle of this handle was moulded a snake, the tail of which twined round at the bottom, while its head with open mouth reached down from the top towards the mouth of the vessel as though in the act of drinking.[1] With this object was associated

[1] Pl. IIIb.

a very large libation bowl ; and these, as well as other features of the deposit, suggest a group of sacred vessels. The snake was in fact a terrestrial emblem of the Mother-goddess, symbolizing Life within the Earth. Even to-day snakes are held sacred in some remote places. On the desert border behind Esneh on the Upper Nile, where we excavated in 1905, the villagers were so terrorized by a pair of great vipers which lived in the adjoining tombs, that they made a practice of appeasing them with saucers of milk placed outside their house-doors at night. They were almost indignant when we finally rid them of these dangerous tyrants, fearing vaguely some evil consequence.

Other modelled devices in pottery appear on two vases, one shaped like a bird, the other like the head of a deer, both supported upon pedestals. Unfortunately, like nearly all the contents of these rooms, these objects were found in fragments. The snake-chalice described above was repaired in our laboratory from no fewer than 73 pieces ; but the trouble was well rewarded.

While the Palace store-rooms illustrated so plentifully the styles of pottery made or selected for special purposes, a more complete series of the forms in common use was provided by an examination of the contemporary tombs. These were usually of the grotto-class, with an open shaft giving access to a subterranean chamber, which, being roofed with a natural vault of rock, had given protection to their contents. Numerous tombs were examined, and they yielded more than a thousand pottery and other specimens mostly in good condition. Here again the pottery vessels,

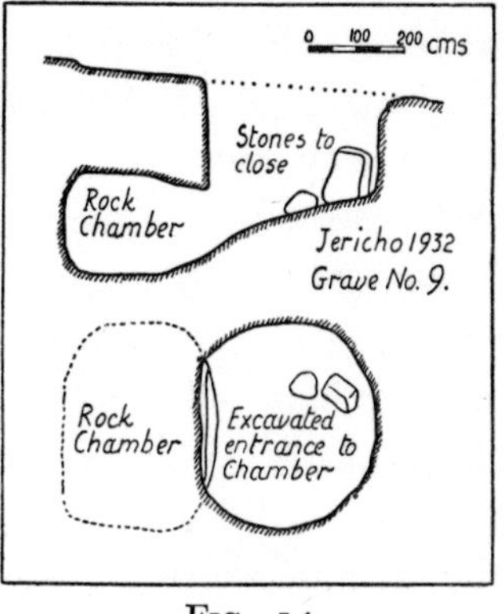

FIG. 14.
Section of a Hyksos Tomb.

though for the most part undecorated, reveal by their elegance and variety of form, no less than their perfection of finish and technique, the stimulus

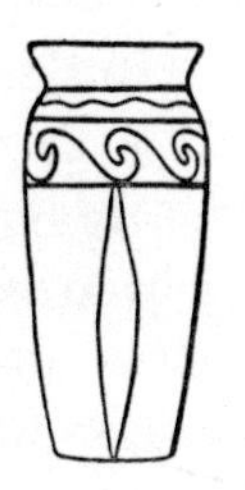
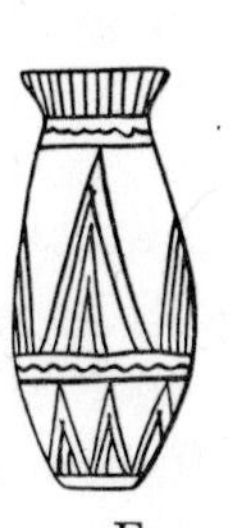
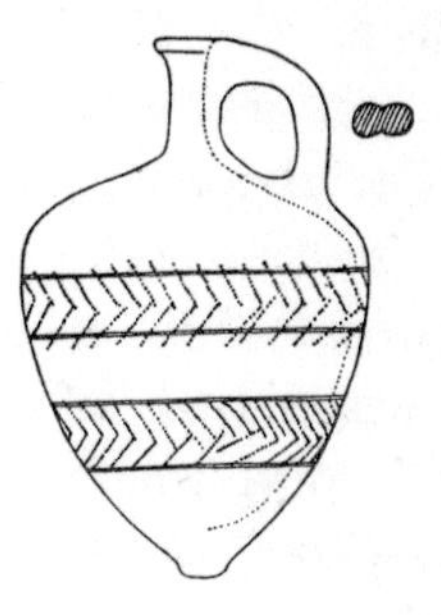

FIG. 15.
Examples of Hyksos Art (City III).

of artistic pride. They were made on a quick wheel, and are remarkable for the refinement of the clay and the smoothness of the finished surface.

Specially attractive are the drinking goblets upon pedestals with broad outcurving rims. Characteristic, too, are the "metallic" forms (with angular profiles) covered with white or creamy slip, thinly worked in refined potter's clay and hard-baked : they ring like a piece of metal. As painted motifs are rare in any class, it was evidently the ambition of the potter to produce a finished product of his own art ; and some of the examples are as near perfection as the Bronze Age ever saw.

Among the objects of exceptional interest found in these tombs may be singled out (from tomb 9) a human-headed drinking vase, or rhyton,[1] dating from the 17th Century B.C. It represents the head of a bearded man, almost life size ; the hairs of his *barbiche* beard are indicated by pin-holes, and there are traces of paint around the eyes and at the back of the neck. The nose is of the Armeno-Hittite type grotesquely exaggerated and starting from the forehead ; while the eyes, which are unnaturally large, are also modelled in the clay. The ears are drawn out sideways to serve as handles. Notwithstanding its grotesque features, this face presumably represents—if only in caricature—a known type of the day ; it is therefore a matter of great interest to note that a very similar one appears, on a vase of different shape, among the discoveries made at Brak in Mesopotamia[2] by Mr. Mallowan, who classes it as an example of Kassite-Babylonian art of about 1500 B.C. The

[1] Pl. XIVa.
[2] Published in the *Illustrated London News* of Jan. 15, 1938.

PLATE XIII

Finished Pottery Styles of Hyksos Period

PLATE XIV

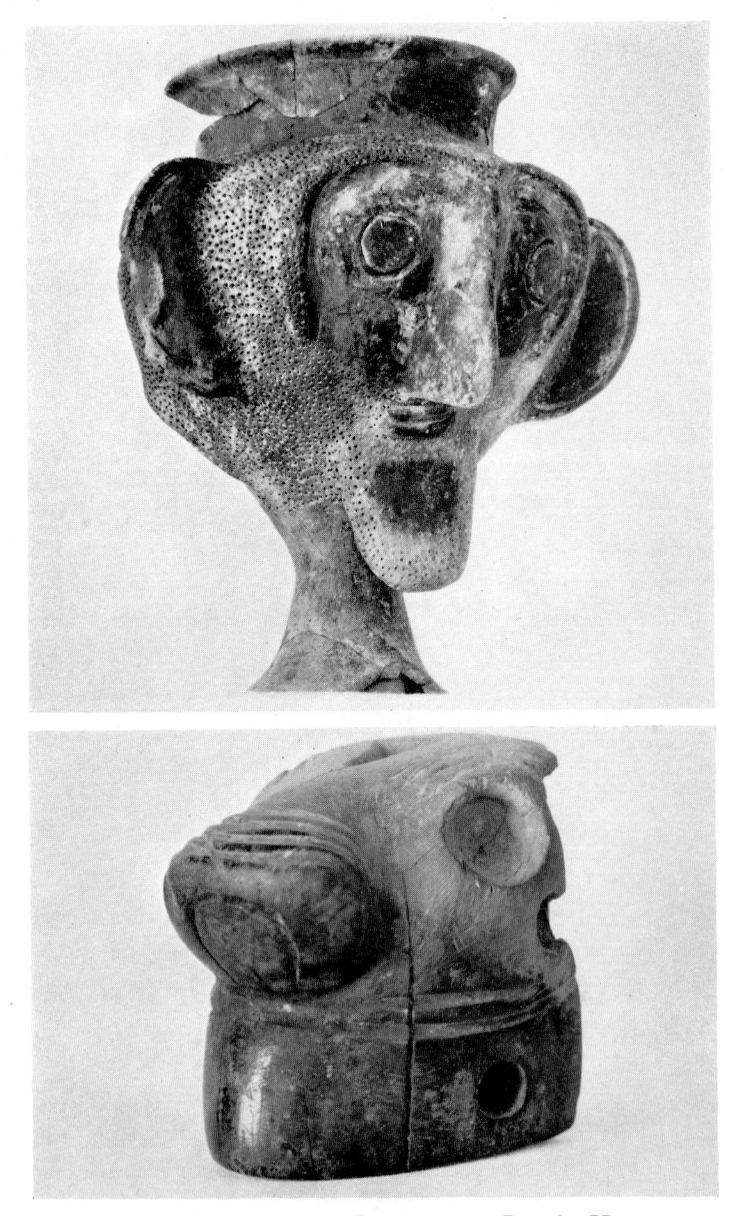

HYKSOS RHYTON AND BABYLONIAN BULL'S HEAD

object is so rare and the parallelism so striking, that it suggests a link connecting the Hyksos invasion of Palestine and Egypt with the Kassite invasion and domination of Babylonia, which began about the same time, and was still effective at the later date of the Brak specimen.

The same tomb also yielded, in addition to further examples of fine pottery, a series of objects in bronze, among which a number of brooches, hair pins with ornamental knobs, and toggle pins are instructive. The latter were used for attaching the loose end of the toga-like outer garment of the day, well seen on one of the decorated scarabs[1] of this period. The " rhyton " tomb (No. 9) yielded up nine scarabs, and also a whole group of bronze implements, among which are a curving knife blade, several daggers with knob attachments of limestone for the butts of the handles, and one fine battle axe furnished with a moulded hook to facilitate the hafting of its shaft.

Scarabs, which were in common use at the time, were found in abundance. These in their origin were seals, and those which bear personal or royal names may be regarded as still fulfilling their purpose. In the East to-day contracts and documents are " signed " by the parties concerned with their seals when they cannot write, and even in preference to writing. Those which show only patterns and conventional devices, whatever may have been their original purpose, were probably used as ornaments or set as rings. But the Royal

[1] Fig. 11.

scarabs, those in particular which bore Hyksos rulers' or Pharaohs' names, were of different character: they were at once the Symbol and the Seal of Office. The investiture of a vassal or of a high official with such a Signet was observed in Egypt as an important ceremony. The case of Joseph provides a good example:

> "*Pharaoh said unto Joseph, See, I have set thee over all the land of Egypt. And Pharaoh took off his signet ring from his hand, and put it upon Joseph's hand.*" (Genesis xli, 41-42.)

The extreme rarity and lack of duplication of such scarabs among the personalities of Jericho buried in the tombs (all of which were scrupulously examined, even to the sieving of the earth) is a clear indication that they were in fact here the emblem of a Royal Mandate.

Among the many scarabs of the Hyksos period

FIG. 16.
Scarabs of Kames and A-kha.

found in our excavations, we should note particularly one royal name, "Nub, King of the North." From the fact that the scarabs of this Hyksos king were found both in the Palace area and in the tomb, it seems probable that he resided in person at one time in Jericho and there died. We find also the names of two other Hyksos chieftains upon the royal scarabs from these tombs, as well as that of a local King of Jericho, named A-kha, who seems to have held office immediately after the Hyksos regime. Most instructive historically is one (from tomb 31) inscribed with the name of the Egyptian king Kames, who was the first to lead the Egyptians in revolt against their Hyksos overlords. The presence of this king's name shows that the Hyksos stores at Jericho were not overlooked by the avenging Egyptian armies.

The Hyksos rule could not last for ever. The "shepherd kings" had lorded it over Egypt for more than a hundred years (1750-1600 B.C.), but the Egyptians, with their proud history and traditions, then revolted against these alien rulers. A movement was set on foot, led by King Kames, to restore the old Theban line of Pharaohs, and in the end the Hyksos were driven out of the country. A new Pharaoh came to the throne, who "knew not Joseph", and a new era had begun.

The fate of Jericho, which had played so definite a part in the Hyksos movement, was now sealed. The Egyptian armies, flushed with success, pursued the hated aliens as far from their borders as possible. The Hyksos retreated whence they had come—in the direction of Syria—and thus Canaan became the battle-ground for a war of liberation and revenge.

In spite of its isolated position, Jericho did not

escape the threatening disaster, and, deserted by the retreating Hyksos, it seems to have been taken by storm by the victorious Egyptians and totally destroyed. In the lack of any direct written allusion to this event, it remains a matter of inference from our observations. But we know that at this time (about 1600 B.C.) part of the northern fosse was filled up (cf. p. 32) as though to facilitate an assault upon the giant ramparts, and that the houses and Palace store-rooms were burnt in a general conflagration.

Traces of this widespread fire were indeed to be found over all the rooms of this period which we examined. In some near the Palace the pottery and other objects were found buried in white ash, which was closely overlaid by a thick layer of charcoal and burnt debris. In many jars the grain was found carbonised, not merely blackened as usual with age. Indeed the store-rooms first found were thought by the workmen to be pottery kilns, and became known as " The Kilns " amongst ourselves, so conspicuous were the traces of fire and so complete the burning of the contents. Charred ends of a number of roofing beams found in one room, coupled with the inflammable nature of the stores, explain the violence of the conflagration.

So perished, once again, the City of Jericho, the third and greatest of the series that arose in turn and fell to ruins upon this now historic site.

CHAPTER VI

JERICHO UNDER EGYPT

Middle and Late Bronze Age: 1600–1400 B.C.

CHAPTER VI

SO devastating were the effects of the destruction and burning of Jericho at the end of the Hyksos rule, that the new City which appeared during the next generation shrank back to the original and narrow limits upon the hill. The population, though greatly reduced in numbers, seems none the less to have remained essentially the same ; this may be inferred from the continuity of the fundamental arts and customs, including burial practices and religion. Their culture in a word was modified only faintly by the Egyptian impact, and the normal life of the community seems to have been soon resumed on a more modest scale. There is indeed a suggestion, from the position and relation of certain scarab signets, that the local king A-kha may have managed to secure the confidence of his Egyptian overlord and so retain his position and authority. All the same the lot of the people of Jericho must have been disquieting, for the country was in turmoil and inevitably it took some time, after so great a political upheaval, before the reorganization of the country became effective and order again prevailed.

The earlier Pharaohs of the re-established dynasty of Egypt were, in fact, fully occupied with following up their victories, and so laying the foundations of their imperial greatness, by a series of far-reaching expeditions in the north: these required the maintenance of the main highways in that direction, but left Jericho out of the picture. The war-harassed cities elsewhere in Canaan were constrained to secure their freedom at a price; and they remained unmolested only so long as they paid their tribute to the Pharaoh and *largesse* to his soldiers. The lists of such "tribute," including prisoners and women carried off as slaves, which decorate the temple walls at Thebes, tell plainly of spoliation and revenge, and explain the rapid impoverishment of the country. Once again Jericho seems to have profited by its isolation, in that it escaped the full effects of such desolating raids and the prevailing lawlessness. The Palace was rebuilt, some of the royal store-rooms were reconstructed, and the restoration of the inner line of fortifications was put in hand.

The Fourth City thus emerged under very difficult conditions; and it is not surprising that special attention was paid to its defences. When completed these enclosed the top of the mound with a double wall of brick, the inner one of which followed and in places actually rested on the old wall of the Second City built during the Early Bronze Age a thousand years before.[1] The outer screen wall was probably retopped at the same time, but in its present ruinous condition

[1] Plates V and XIIb.

we cannot feel certain of the period of its restoration. All this work would certainly require time, and may have been spread over a good part of the century. No use seems to have been made of the old ramparts of the Hyksos period, which were left in their semi-demolished state, while the slopes which had been occupied at that time now remained uninhabited: evidently the older cir-

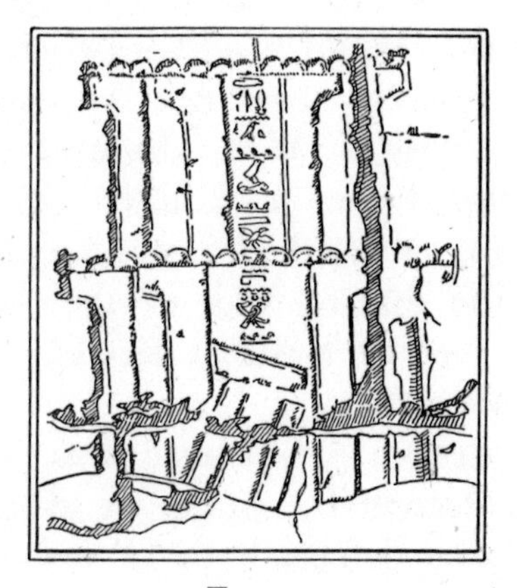

FIG. 17.
Egyptian representation of a city tower falling.

cuit round the brink of the mound sufficed to house the reduced population. The inception of such work, indeed, shows that the city was rapidly reviving; and suffering no further set-backs it began to enjoy a measure of prosperity.

In the completed scheme the old gate-tower on the eastern side became practically obliterated; indeed the line of the new wall used it as a foundation. It was replaced, however, by a new tower in the north-west corner of the enclosure, which embraced both the inner and outer walls and was 90 feet in length. Rising high above the walls at their highest point, this feature dominated not only the City but the surrounding country. Such towers, or "migdols," were characteristic of the age, and figure on Egyptian drawings of Canaanite cities, where they look rather like a fortified "keep" within the outer line of defence. Mural towers supported the other angles, and between these ran the curtain of the outer wall. Within, at a distance of four or five yards, ran the main or inner wall, a massive brick structure 12 feet thick: standing for the most part upon the disused wall of the Second City, it probably rose at least 20 feet in clear height on the outside.

This impressive appearance was, however, to some extent deceptive. Although so massive, this new wall shows defects both of material and in construction. As usual the bricks of which it was built were merely sun-dried, not kiln-baked, and contained no binding straw. They were small and of unequal size, though an average thickness of four inches was fairly well maintained. They are distinctly warm in colour, hence containing possibly more earth and less clay, as compared with the solid yellow bricks of the underlying structure; and it is remarkable how much more they now show signs of wear and weakness. Moreover the foundations were irregular. The old wall upon which they partly rested had not been trued up continuously before the new work began ; so that where there were hollows or where the two lines did not coincide, the gaps were filled (in some cases only partially) by a layer of field stones, laid upon the accumulated debris. Such weak spots in the foundations of a wall so weighty as this would not only make it difficult for the builders to keep the courses regular, but be likely to induce subsidence. Examples may be seen in our photograph on Pl. XVII, and the measured diagram on Pl. XVIII ; in which it should also be noted that this defect appears on the outer side, towards the slope of the mound.

A further source of weakness arose from the building of houses against or actually upon the walls. They crowded thickly against the inner face of the main wall, and on the north and west were built high above the normal town level, upon foundations provided by narrow cross-walls that bonded the ramparts together, and timbers that bridged the intervening space. The need for building-room within the cramped limits of the new city had evidently become acute with the increased numbers and prosperity of the community under Egyptian protection, and in this age of apparent security overpowered military considerations ; for these dwellings would be a serious hindrance to the defenders in a siege, besides tending to put an undue stress from within upon the overloaded and untrustworthy foundations.

The "culture" of the place during the century which ensued, as illustrated by the contents of the tombs and store-rooms, was still derived from that of the Hyksos period, of which it forms the latest phase. The survival of local art and customs is well illustrated by discoveries in the necropolis, where some of the tombs contained interments of the Third and Fourth Cities without trace of any interruption; in fact few tombs belonged only to the Fourth City. Scarab-seals found in the tomb of the Rhyton-vase (No. 9) already described give ready evidence of this continuity (cf. Pl. XV); some of these belong to the purely Hyksos period of the 17th Century B.C., but others, though still of Hyksos character, fall definitely within the First Century of Egyptian domination. The other objects found in this burial grotto are equally separable into earlier and later phases of a common style.

"Tomb 5," which we shall find of increasing interest in the later story of the city, also adds convincing evidence of like kind, though itself an open grave, in contrast to the grotto type described above. The pottery sequence is in this case complete all through the Middle Bronze Age styles of the Third and Fourth Cities, and it even carries the link onwards into the Late Bronze Age, as far as the end of the 15th Century B.C. The objects in this tomb were closely packed and indeed so numerous (613 to be precise) that seven layers in all were removed by the excavators. It should be explained in passing

PLATE XV

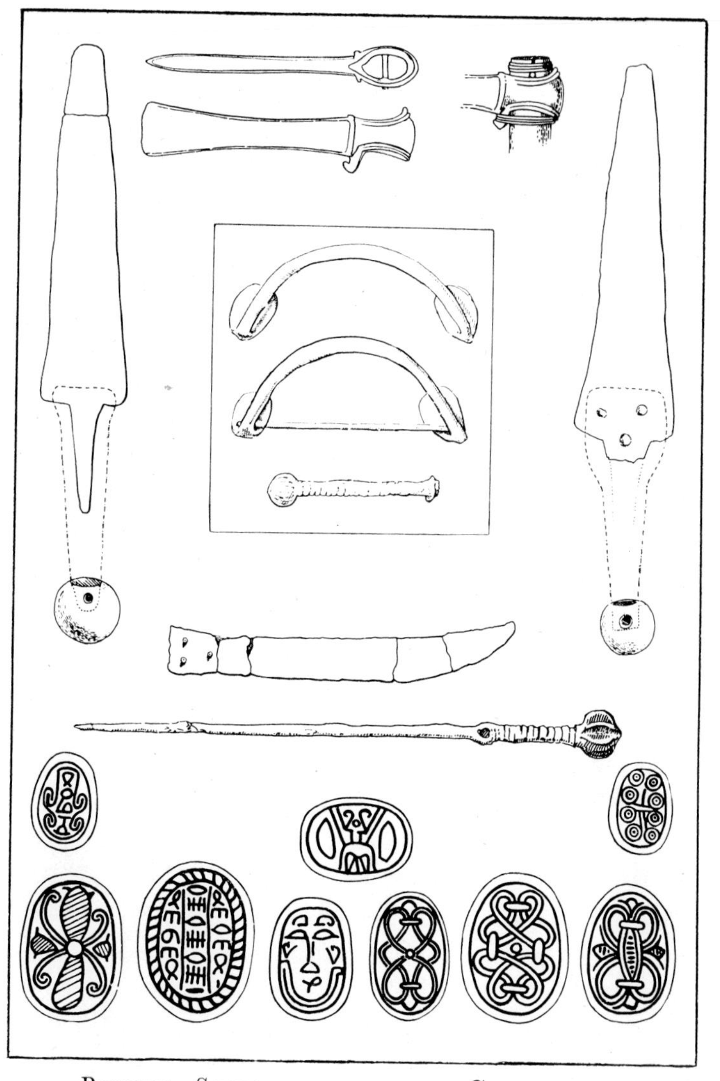

BRONZES, SCARABS, ETC.: 17TH CENTURY B.C.

PLATE XVI

Residence of the Last Kings of Jericho: and Storerooms of the Hyksos Palace

that such "layers" of deposits in tombs are not separated from one another like the "levels of occupation" of a city; they merely describe the regular way in which the objects accumulated within the tombs as generations passed, though speaking generally the lowest "layers" will also be the earliest. Tomb 5 was actually interesting for many reasons other than the number of its vases, as will be seen in the following pages.

Within the city itself evidence as to this phase was almost entirely limited (by the effects of previous excavations) to the contents of two or three house-rooms against the city walls and some of the restored store-rooms of the Palace area. In some of these the floor levels had been raised at the time of reconstruction above the accumulated debris, so that the upper deposits remained distinct from those below, except for a number of vessels saved from the great fire and brought up for re-use. The evidence, though limited, was then quite reliable, and it confirmed the continuity of the Hyksos culture illustrated so clearly in the tombs.

LAST PHASE OF THE FOURTH CITY: (LATE BRONZE AGE). It was not until the 15th Century B.C. was well advanced that a marked cultural change heralded the Late Bronze Age, which here as elsewhere in Canaan followed in the wake of the Egyptian conquests by opening the door to the expanding trade relations of the Pharaohs' empire. Hitherto, as already explained, Jericho had lain outside their imperial scheme;

but about 1475 B.C. Thothmes III took effective control of the city. Following up the sack of Megiddo (about 1478 B.C.) by a series of irresistible campaigns he established Egypt's firm dominion throughout the country; and the association of his predecessor Queen Hatshepsut's scarab with his own (in Tomb 5) points to a date early in the series for the formal annexation of Jericho. There is no reason to suppose that the local king or people opposed this step—rather the reverse. The somewhat tardy assertion of the Pharaoh's authority at Jericho was probably due to its isolation and its relative unimportance hitherto

FIG. 18.
Royal Egyptian Scarab Signets of the last Kings of Jericho.

in the imperial scheme. But Thothmes III was not only an energetic and successful military leader but a great organizer, and he sealed his conquests by setting up an effective system of administration. Under him the Egyptians became in fact conscious of their Empire, and in the new scheme the chieftains of important Canaanite cities became the Pharaoh's representatives, while Egyptian Residents were established at Gaza and other chosen centres. Numerous petitions and reports from such chieftains, addressed to later Pharaohs, have been discovered in Egypt, and constitute the famous Amarna Letters.

At Jericho the local king was now installed as a vassal of the Pharaoh, and the imperial signet rings have actually been found in "Tomb 5", which thus is revealed as the burial place of the new royal family. The king's official duties would be to secure the Pharaoh's interest in his district, to repress native discontent and foreign intrigue (which was abundant), to collect and forward the due quota of tribute; to assist the state

FIG. 19.
Foreign Deity on the back of an animal.

couriers on their journeyings and to prepare when necessary for the lodging and victualling of troops setting out on campaign. The latter obligation had hitherto been light, for the Pharaohs of the 17th Century had been busied in the conquest of the north; now, presumably, the Egyptian tentacles were spreading eastward towards the cornlands beyond Jordan.

To support the king's authority and no doubt

(in Oriental fashion) to keep an eye upon his own doings, a small garrison of foreign soldiers seems now to have been established within the city: this is to be inferred from the contents of a cremation pit, discovered on the border of the necropolis, in which were found a scarab of Thothmes III and another of later date bearing the picture of a foreign deity upon the back of an animal. The indications in this case are insufficient to determine the origins of the new guards. It should be mentioned that such "garrisons" are not to be visualized in our conception of the word; for they generally consisted of only two or three (at the most five) well armed mercenaries, usually "Sherdens".

In the excavation of the last Hyksos Palace and its adjoining store-rooms we noted the traces of earthquake and extensive burning. It will be remembered (from Chapter III) that Jericho had previously suffered the consequences of its dangerous position in the Rift, and during the 15th Century B.C. it was again severely damaged by another such catastrophe. The traces are unmistakable: one of the Palace walls was broken in two, and the brickwork of this and other walls was brought toppling down in large masses. Local fires broke out and completed the disaster, charring and cracking the bricks and the contents of the surviving store-rooms.

Thanks possibly to the now active interest of Egypt in the city, the task of repairing the damage was put in hand without much delay. The outer wall in particular, which it will be remembered stood somewhat down the slope, was strengthened in places with an added revetment of stone, and the great tower or migdol seems to have been retopped with smaller bricks and consolidated with a central core. Most houses of this period within the walls were found so denuded that it was impossible to trace the signs of reconstruction; but fortunately good evidence was forthcoming from the old Palace area on the central knoll overlooking the spring. There we found that the Hyksos Palace itself was not rebuilt after this earthquake: the royal family seem to have lived in a new and smaller building[1] of different character lower down the slope over the site of the old store-rooms. In plan this house comprised a courtyard and five rooms, two of which were much larger than the others; and the whole seems to have been enclosed by a stout wall of stone, built however at different times.

Though in general the remains of this building and even its destruction layer were well preserved, it was found unfortunately to have been much disturbed in places by the foundations of a stout building of later date (the block-house described on p. 146), which had penetrated deeply into the lower levels, even as far as the Hyksos Palace (cf. Fig. 4). Investigation was further complicated by the fact that the rooms of the upper building had been largely cleared before our work began, so that the deposits had become mixed, with the result that

[1] 2 in Fig. 4; also Pl. XVIa.

the items of evidence have required careful sifting and prolonged study in order to deduce from them reliable historical conclusions.

The pottery properly belonging to this building (including new styles and painted fabrics) corresponds exactly with the later specimens from " tomb 5 " already mentioned, which made their first appearance soon after the scarabs of Queen Hatshepsut and Thothmes III. It is also linked by individual examples with the later deposits of the store-rooms of the previous generation ; and from this evidence it is clear that the Egyptian annexation, while opening up trade-relations with other parts of the Empire, such as Cyprus, did not cause any violent interruption in the local arts and religious practices of the community. This new pottery also finds its counterparts among specimens from the corresponding levels at Beisan, where again the later Hyksos styles give way in similar fashion to the fresh motifs which are characteristic of the latter half of the 15th Century B.C.

Pottery of the Late Bronze Age differs in many features from the earlier wares. The angular (carinated) shapes and goblets have disappeared ; while painted decoration, which was rare before, becomes now quite common, with a leaning to particular motifs. Foreign wares, too, are now imported to a greater extent, and also imitated by local craftsmen. Such wares include Cypriote and Syro-Phœnician vessels, for instance milk-bowls with " wish-bone " handles, and " bilbils "

—a digger's name for a special jug with pipe-like neck—both types familiar in the Egyptian world during the 16th and 15th Centuries B.C. It is noteworthy (as we shall have occasion to see later) how little trace there is of Mycenæan pottery from the Helladic world, the importation of which began generally about 1400 B.C. : indeed only one small fragment has been found inside

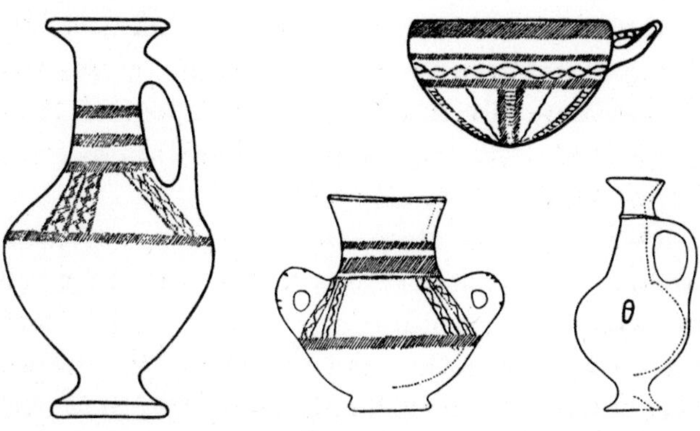

FIG. 20.
Late Bronze Age Pottery of City IV : c. 1475 B.C.

the city where we examined more than 150,000 pieces ; while elsewhere in the tombs or outside the city such specimens as have been observed are the imitations of a later age not represented within the city's walls.

Other objects of special interest found in the excavation of this building include a figure of the goddess Astarte and a tablet with cuneiform writing. The inscription of the latter cannot be read intelligibly as it is much damaged by fire, and some of the signs seem originally to have been bungled or left incomplete as though done in haste. It is just possible to read the first sign to mean " Hebrews " (*Habiru*), but the best scholars regard this interpretation as unlikely. The bad state of this document is most unfortunate, especially as a reasonably complete inscription at this level might have furnished direct evidence as to the date of the city's fall.

WHEN WAS THE FOURTH CITY DESTROYED? This is an important question, because on its correct solution depends the whole chronological framework of the early history of the Israelites as related in the Bible.

The evidence from the city alone does not provide a complete answer, but taken in conjunction with the parallel evidence of the tombs it becomes decisive. For in these the deposits were dated and continuous from the time when Thothmes III annexed the city (c. 1475 B.C.) until the reign of Amenhetep III. This Pharaoh ruled alone from 1412 till 1385 B.C., but a date towards the end of this period is indicated by the discovery (in tomb 4) of two of his royal seals, which suggest that two local dynasts had been buried during his reign prior to the city's fall.

We must approach this problem then by linking up the various items of evidence from within the city and comparing them with the dated materials from the tombs. Though the manner in which the walls fell was plainly illustrated, separate evidence as to the date of that event is meagre. There was found, however, sufficient indication that the main walls and the buildings abutting against them perished at the same time and from the same cause.

Examination of certain areas which had not been disturbed, stretches of wall under tip-heaps and a few other places not previously excavated, showed plainly that the defending wall had been completely moved from its foundations and that intense fire while completing its destruction had involved some adjoining rooms. A few things rescued from the debris of ash and charcoal in one ruin told plainly of a household cut off in full activity, and the broken pottery should therefore give a clue to the approximate date of the catastrophe.

Such archæological remains as were found in these rooms, however, though they included distinctive pieces like the "wish-bone" handles of Cypriote fabric, and a few painted potsherds, both current in the 15th Century B.C., were of too long a range to supply a precise answer to our question. They came however within the classes of wares abundantly represented in the area and rooms of the later Palace already described, and it becomes clear that this building also perished in the general conflagration that destroyed the city as a whole. The dating of the latest parallel deposits in tombs 4 and 5, happily provided by the royal scarabs independently of external considerations, will thus complete the answer to our question. The date when the

Fourth City was destroyed may fall as late as 1385 B.C., but no later, for neither in tombs nor city was anything found that could be ascribed to the time of Akhenaton (the "Heretic King"), who began to reign independently about 1375 B.C., having apparently shared the throne since 1384 with his father Amenhetep III.

The art of the great reformer's reign is distinctive and well-known, but none of it appears at Jericho. Moreover his reign saw a great influx from the Greek world of Mycenæan wares: a trading depôt of the period has actually been found in Palestine near the port of Haifa, and it was rich in these wares, of which however only one fragment has been found within the walls of Jericho. The age of Akhenaton is thus not represented at all by the material remains unearthed; and this indication accords with the fact that the name of Jericho nowhere appears in the Amarna letters, which refer frequently to most of the great cities of Palestine, such as Gaza, Gath, Jerusalem, Shechem, Megiddo, Akko, and possibly even to incidents in the Jordan valley. The inference is obvious, that, unless by some curious coincidence all tablets referring to Jericho have been lost, this city no longer claimed attention, that it was in fact already in ruins at the time of this official correspondence. This interpretation is confirmed by the evidence of the scarabs, the long series of which ends with the reign of Amenhetep III.

The circumstantial evidence is thus all in

complete agreement, so that any odds and ends of pottery (and they are few) which belong to subsequent generations only tell of a partial or casual occupation of the site.

It should be added, since the fact might seem to argue a later date, that a complete vase of late Mycenæan type (the date of which ranges from 1300 to 1200 B.C.) was found outside the old Hyksos ramparts[1] against which a few late houses had been built at a time when the rest of the city

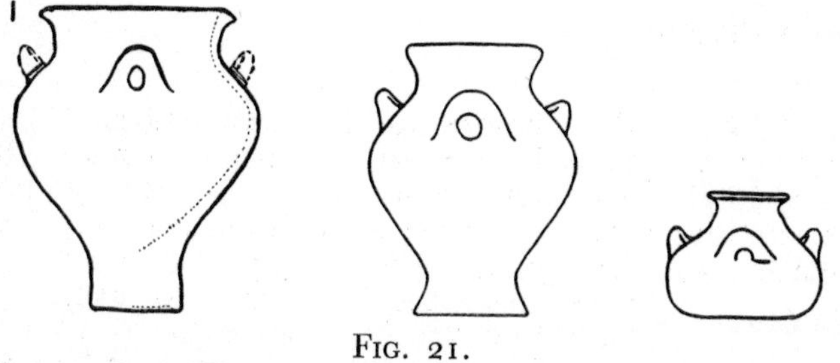

FIG. 21.
Late Mycenæan Pottery from Tomb 13.

was in ruins. Actually it lay sandwiched between a layer of burnt matter from the holocaust in which the Fourth City perished and another layer of ashes from the destruction of the houses themselves. It must therefore have arrived at the site some time after Jericho fell, and may be classed in this general respect with half a dozen pots, three of them imitations of Mycenæan shapes, which were found in the upper layer of a re-used tomb (No. 13) where they were a recognizably intrusive element. These, if they are to

[1] MP in Fig. 2.

be dated to a later age (which is not certain since their range was wide), would confirm the presence of casual settlers on the deserted site but afford no evidence as to the date when it became desolate.

This date, we repeat, may be fixed with considerable assurance, as a glance at the statistical contents of the tombs is alone sufficient to indicate. From 43 tombs examined, of which 26 contained pottery, we get the following quantitative results, noting that a few tombs only of the first period were discovered :

First City:	Early Bronze Age, i	(3000-2500 B.C.)	55
Second City:	Early Bronze Age, ii	(2500-2000 B.C.)	891
Third City:	Middle Bronze Age, ii	(1900-1600 B.C.)	1,012
Fourth City, i:	Middle Bronze Age, iii	(1600-1500 B.C.)	519
Fourth City, ii:	Late Bronze Age, i	(1500-1385 B.C.)	320
No City:	Late Bronze Age, ii	(1385-1200 B.C.)	8
	Early Iron Age, i	(1200-900 B.C.)	14
Fifth City:	Early Iron Age, ii	(900-700 B.C.)	No tombs

This table tells its own story ; and it is in full agreement with our observations in the city itself, where however the individual pots could not be counted as they were mostly smashed to fragments. It shows that the active life of the city and its burial practices came to a sudden end at one and the same time. The 500 years that preceded this event are represented by 1,800 objects ; the subsequent 500 years by 22.

The evidence may then be summarized as follows. On the one hand both in the city and in the tombs we have an abundant and parallel series of pottery and scarabs covering the reigns of the Pharaohs from Thothmes III to Amenhetep III—the single fragment of Mycenæan pottery from the city is early and may be assigned to the last of these. On the other hand neither in the City nor in the tombs did we discover any objects datable to the reign of Akhenaton, though Mycenæan pottery of the later styles (13th and 12th Centuries B.C.), found in the tombs and beside the mound, attests a partial reoccupation of the site some considerable time after his death. This combination of positive and negative evidence establishes a verdict which is at once logical and final: the Fourth City was destroyed after 1400 and before 1385 B.C.

CHAPTER VII

THE CITY DESTROYED BY JOSHUA

(*1400–1388 B.C.*)

CHAPTER VII

THE patient reader who has followed us thus far in our examination of Jericho through the Ages of antiquity is entitled now to ask at what stage and how the Bible narrative fits into this outline.

Having set down the facts as we observed them, and stated our main conclusions, we are in a safe position to examine this aspect of our subject. This will probably appeal to most readers more strongly than the preceding archæological enquiry, yet we have pursued this course, as we did throughout the excavations, with a purpose. Much of the work done in the Holy Land has been stripped of its scientific value by the assumption that the Scriptures are above criticism and necessarily exact in every detail. Yet generations of scholars have examined the structure of the Book: they have told us that, whatever may have been its original nucleus, it was added to, modified, and edited throughout successive centuries, and that the very documents constituting the Bible as now translated are comparatively recent copies made devotedly by hand, but liable for that reason also to contain mistakes. Accordingly students to-day claim the right to form their own opinions, and it is the archæologist's duty to present the evidence as free from prejudice and colouration as is humanly possible when personal faith and beliefs are involved. In the search for Truth the only safe procedure in such a case, we submit, is to present the facts first, and then to examine the relevant passages in the Bible, to see to what extent they agree or disagree with the material evidence, and whatever the result to state it without prejudice or concealment.

THE BIBLICAL DATE. It has been shown that, prior to the fall of the Fourth City, Jericho had been already twice partly or wholly destroyed and burnt within a space of about two hundred years. Our first point will be to decide which of these cities, if any, can have been that which Joshua and the Israelites are said to have annihilated. Such an enquiry must consider not only the date, but the appearance of special features of the city at that time, the manner of its destruction and the political circumstances of the Age.

In the Bible unfortunately there is no direct indication of the date at which Jericho was destroyed by Joshua, but we possess a clear lead to it in the statement made in I Kings, vi, 1:

> "*In the four hundred and eightieth year after the children of Israel were come out of the land of Egypt, in the fourth year of Solomon's reign over Israel . . . he began to build the house of the Lord.*"

In other words, according to the Israelites' own traditions, the period of their history from the time they left Egypt until the fourth year of Solomon's reign (known from other sources to have fallen about 967 B.C.) covered 480 years. Now the figure 480 is a round one, based on the method of measuring broad intervals by periods of forty years,[1] much as we might use the word "generation". Though probably not giving us an exact figure it may be assumed to aim at accuracy within the broad margin of 20 years on each side: it will indicate, then, in this case something between 461 and 499 years. This figure includes both the duration of the Exodus from Egypt and the sojourn of the Israelites in the wilderness prior to their entry into the Promised Land, the latter again being estimated on the same basis at 40 years. The date of the destruction of Jericho would thus fall about 440 years before 967 B.C., i.e. about 1407 B.C., not earlier than 1426 nor later than 1388 B.C.

These dates nearly cover the extreme limits within which the Fourth City of Jericho can have been destroyed upon the evidence of our excavations; indeed any year between 1400 and 1388 B.C. will satisfy both sources. The accordance as to date is thus very close; and there is an *a priori* case for comparing the relevant details of the narrative with what is known of the Fourth City in its last phase and the manner of its destruction.

THE FOURTH CITY. An artist's impression of this City, based on the results of the excavations, is reproduced as our Frontispiece. This view is from the East as Jericho would be approached from

[1] As well seen in the chronological scheme of the Book of Judges. Cf. *Joshua, Judges*, p. 65.

the fords of the Jordan, and in the foreground is the ever-flowing stream. Beyond it the mound, now much higher than of old, rises from the gate steeply towards the west, where the clustered houses are shown piled and encroaching upon the main rampart. In the middle of the City, on " Spring-hill ", is seen the knoll beneath which the former palaces of its great days lie buried, and on the near side stands the house of Jericho's last king, within full view and control of the entrance. Nearby to the south-west is placed conjecturally the temple of Astarte, the Nature-goddess. Elsewhere most of the enclosed area of four or five acres is packed with small houses ; and surrounding all are the defensive walls, imposingly placed on the brink of the steep slopes, the foot of which is still marked by the half-filled fosse and crumbling ramparts of the Third City.

These new walls, though not more than 250 yards in length from north to south, and 100 yards along the shorter sides, must indeed have presented a formidable appearance to attackers. They stood high upon those of the Second City, each corner being strengthened by a solid mural bastion 20 feet in thickness ; and in spite of the flaws which we have noted in their construction, the fact that they could support rooms and houses in the way described in the last chapter is a sufficient indication of their solidity, while the very thickness of the inner wall under normal circumstances ought to have been equal to the imposed strain. But the inhabitants, already afraid of the super-

PLATE XVII

THE FALLEN WALLS OF CITY IV (1400-1385 B.C.)

PLATE XVIII

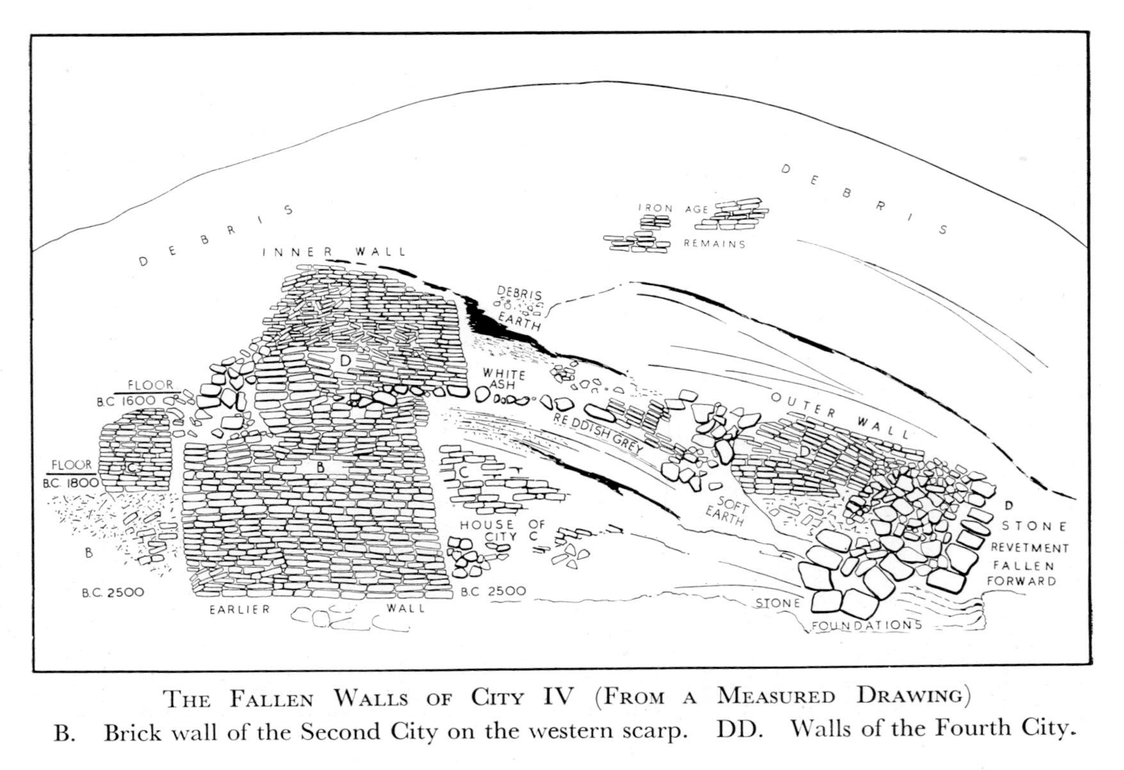

THE FALLEN WALLS OF CITY IV (FROM A MEASURED DRAWING)

B. Brick wall of the Second City on the western scarp. DD. Walls of the Fourth City.

human aid said to have been given to the Israelite invaders, were suddenly brought face to face with a manifestation of that power, which this time overwhelmed the city in a final destruction.

HOW THE WALLS FELL. The visible effects of this catastrophe were summarized in a field report (dated March 2nd, 1930) endorsed by brother archæologists from which we quote the following description : " The main defences of Jericho in the Late Bronze Age followed the upper brink of the city mound, and comprised two parallel walls, the outer six feet and the inner twelve feet thick. Investigations along the west side show continuous signs of destruction and conflagration. The outer wall suffered most, its remains falling down the slope. The inner wall is preserved only where it abuts upon the citadel, or tower, to a height of eighteen feet ; elsewhere it is found largely to have fallen, together with the remains of buildings upon it, into the space between the walls which was filled with ruins and debris. Traces of intense fire are plain to see, including reddened masses of brick, cracked stones, charred timbers and ashes. Houses alongside the wall were found burnt to the ground, their roofs fallen upon the domestic pottery within."

The north and south walls were already largely denuded before our excavations began, while the east wall near the spring had disappeared almost completely : for these reasons it was not until the second year of our work that we came upon the evidences described, while cautiously tracing the western wall beneath the pile of ruins and later debris. Until then we had thought it possible that the outer wall might have been undermined, an impression created by the fact that the fallen stones of the revetment, resting on debris, simulated disturbed foundations. It is not easy to probe to the bottom of a fallen wall and to leave the wall itself in place ; and we were very unwilling to disturb any of the scanty evidence remaining. In the end, however, we succeeded in obtaining the complete section (reproduced on Pl. XVIII), which shows the stone foundations of both the inner and outer walls to be almost in place upon their undisturbed bed of earth. This ruled out finally the theory of undermining, and further investigations confirmed this conclusion.

WHY THE WALLS FELL. What then could account for so stupendous a catastrophe ? In the first place we can discuss in a few lines various quaint theories which sometimes appear in print. One ingeniously urges that the Israelites made the walls of Jericho fall down by the rhythmic tramping of their feet ; and in support of this it is pointed out that troops nowadays are encouraged to " break step " when going over a bridge. It is not easy, however, to picture Joshua and the Israelites, fresh from the deserts, as marching in measured step or knowing anything of such a ruse. Nor can it be admitted that tramping round the soft mud slopes of Jericho would ever result in even a mild vibration, not to speak of a destructive rhythm. Nor can one take seriously the suggestion that the walls fell because of a loud shout which the Israelites are said to have given. The inner wall, however badly constructed, was four yards thick, and it would need a more-than-human shout to bring it down. For the same reason we can dismiss the theory that the special note of the trumpets blown by the priests was responsible for their collapse : you cannot set up a vibration in a mud-brick wall though you blow till Domesday. One plausible theory, the possibility of undermining, has already been examined and found to be inconsistent with the evidence. Moreover organized siege operations are incompatible with the picture we have of the Israelites, a collection of nomad tribes, who were baffled in their subsequent efforts to capture even the smaller cities of the interior, let alone the strongly fortified places such as Beisan, Taanach, Megiddo and Jerusalem.

One conclusion indeed seems certain : the power that could dislodge hundreds of tons of masonry in the way described must have been superhuman. Earthquake is the one and only known agent capable of the demonstration of force indicated by the observed facts ; and there is reason to believe that in this lies the real answer to our question. Not only does Jericho lie in a volcanic zone which is never wholly free from earthquake shocks, but the evidence of the site itself, as revealed by our excavations, points incontestably to this solution.

Wherever the walls of the Fourth City have been disclosed, they are found to be deeply fissured and as it were dislocated (our photograph on Pl. XVII shows this clearly). These indications point to earthquake, and the native workmen, who have suffered from this cause in the Jordan valley and know the results, interpreted the signs without hesitation. That the walls should have fallen mostly outwards, down the slope, was the natural consequence of its situation and of the defects already described in its foundations on that side.

Volcanic and seismic disturbances have been felt in and around the Jordan Rift at frequent intervals, and the following table shows some of the recorded instances :

1. Stone Age. Earthquake at Jericho (see Pl. IX).
2. About 2000 B.C. Destruction of Sodom and Gomorrah. (Cf. p. 165.)
3. About 1450 B.C. Earthquake at Jericho. (Cf. p. 116.)
4. (?) About 10 B.C. Implied in a story told by Josephus (*Antiq:* Bk. xiv, Chapter xv, 11.)
5. A.D. 1202. Earthquake in Syria and Egypt.
6. A.D. 1204. Earthquake in Western Asia.
7. A.D. 1302. Earthquake in Syria and Egypt.
8. A.D. 1303. Ditto ; Damascus and Acre affected.
9. A.D. 1698. Ditto ; Rosetta and Alexandria affected.
10. A.D. 1837. Earthquake in Palestine ; 4,000 killed at Safed.
11. A.D. 1906. Ditto ; the Jordan temporarily dammed.
12. A.D. 1927. Violent earthquake across the Rift, with much damage and loss of life in Palestine including Jericho : the Jordan dammed for 21 hours.

It is of great interest to note, in passing, that the last of these earthquakes produced effects upon the Jordan precisely similar to those recorded in the Book of Joshua. On this occasion the high west bank of the river, some twenty miles upstream near the ford at El Damieh, collapsed, carrying with it the roadway ; while just below, a section of the cliff, which here rises to a height of 150 feet, fell bodily across the river and dammed it so that no water flowed down the river bed for nearly a whole day. Meanwhile the rising waters gradually covered the plain on the eastern bank round Tell el Damieh, and so found their way eventually back to the river bed : but it was not for more than twenty-one hours that the temporary barrage was washed away and the river resumed its normal course. In the meanwhile several living witnesses crossed and recrossed the bed of the river freely on foot.

A very similar occurrence is said to have taken place in A.D. 1266 when the Sultan Bibars ordered a bridge to be built across the Jordan in the neighbourhood of Damieh. The task was found to be difficult owing to a flood. "But in the night "preceding the 8th December, 1267, a lofty mound, "which overlooked the river on the west, fell into "it and dammed it up, so that the water of the "river ceased to flow and none remained in its "bed. The water spread over the valley above "the dam and none flowed down the bed for "some sixteen hours." This record is preserved by an Arab historian, by name Nowairi.[1]

The resemblance between these two incidents (particularly that of 1927) and the events described in the book of Joshua is far too close for us to treat

[1] Cf. *P.E.F. Q.S.* 1895, pp. 253-261.

it as a mere coincidence. We read there (Joshua iii, 16):

> "*the waters which came down from above stood and rose up in one heap, a great way off, at Adam, the city that is beside Zaretan: and those that went down toward the sea of the Arabah, even the Salt Sea, were wholly cut off: and the people passed over right against Jericho.*"

This passage points again to El Damieh, which is pronounced Ed Damieh, and presumably is the same place as "Adam" of the narrative.

It follows from these considerations that not only have earthquakes been frequent in the Jordan Rift, but that some of them have produced just those consequences that facilitated the Israelites in their movement towards Jericho, where the fall of the walls can also be fully explained by this and no other known cause. The fuller significance of these indications, as explaining the faith of the Israelites in Jehovah's powers, will become apparent in the next chapter which discusses the Exodus and the happenings on Mount Horeb, to which the Fall of Jericho formed the sequel.

THE CITY BURNT WITH FIRE. Let us return now to the City itself, the buildings inside its walls, and resume the story of its fate. We have already mentioned the discovery of some house-rooms against the western wall, and explained how it was that others could not be found. Though few, these buildings gave consistent and repeated proofs of a general conflagration. In one house which leant against the north-western tower there stood in the corner of a room a grain jar still partly filled with wheat ; this was all charred and some of it was spread over the floor of the room, where also were found the remains of cooking pots and domestic objects blackened and cracked with fire.

In another room abutting upon the same western wall, but more to the south, the traces of fire upon its walls were as fresh as though it had occurred a month before ; each scrape of the trowel exposed a black layer of charcoal, where the roof had burned, or caused the piled up ashes to run down in a stream. On a brick ledge in a corner of this room we found the family provision of dates, barley, oats, olives, an onion and peppercorns, all charred but unmistakable ; while a little store of bread, together with a quantity of unbaked dough which had been laid aside to serve as leaven for the morrow's baking, told plainly the same tale of a people cut off in full activity. The domestic pottery lay about in fragments ; this also was charred and clinked with a metallic ring which betrayed the extra baking it had received.

More extensive indications of like kind were found in the heart of the city, in the mound which overlooks the spring, where under a stout building of later date we discovered the ruins of the last king's " palace." Here the destruction-layer was in places plainly visible and undisturbed, and we were able to examine it in detail. The royal residence had been burnt, and lay buried knee deep in white ash and charred debris. One gets used to " burnt layers " in excavations of this kind, for it was the usual fate of houses and cities to perish by fire ; but this was no ordinary burning. The layer of ashes was so thick and the signs of intense heat so vivid, that it gave the impression of having been contrived, that fuel had been added to the fire. Amongst the embers were traces of charred reeds and bits of wood : it is true that such materials were employed locally to roof the houses, but here was ten times more than was necessary for that purpose, and traces were equally abundant outside the house areas as within. It was the same between the city walls, where in places the pile of burnt matter was as much as five feet high, and the inner face of the main wall still showed clear signs of the conflagration for several years after it had been exposed. It looks, in short, as though Jericho was finally burnt after deliberate preparation ; that it was in fact devoted as a holocaust, precisely in the manner described in the Book of Joshua :

> " *They burnt the city with fire and all that was therein.*" (vi, 24.)

In addition then to the coincidence in date, another of the points which we set out to examine may be regarded as established, namely that the destruction of the Fourth City corresponds in all material particulars with the Biblical narrative of the Fall of Jericho before the Israelites under Joshua.

THE HISTORICAL BACKGROUND. Our problem

PLATE XIX

GRAIN, DATES AND BREAD FROM A BURNT ROOM OF CITY IV

gains interest ; and before continuing our examination of the Biblical account, in which there still lurks a crucial question, it will be wise at this stage to test the validity of the conclusions already reached from an external standpoint, to examine in fact the historical setting of this episode. Was it possible for the Israelites to have entered Canaan and taken Jericho at the date indicated, unchallenged by the superior forces of Egypt the suzerain power ? Fortunately there is relatively abundant evidence upon this point from the Egyptian records, including the Amarna letters, which were mostly addressed to Akhenaton, but included some appeals to his predecessor Amenhetep III. One among these complains that no Egyptian troops had visited the country for fifty years.

This is direct light upon the historical setting of the fall of Jericho, in which the Biblical account makes no suggestion of succour to the menaced city from Jerusalem and Shechem, the nearest centres of Egyptian authority. Indeed, letters from Abd-Khipa, king of Jerusalem, addressed to the next Pharaoh, appeal for soldiers there against the growing menace ; and this also seems to throw light upon the failure of the league of loyal cities from the south (including Hebron and Lachish) which Adoni-Zedek, probably his successor, summoned to resist the Israelite inroads in the next stage of their advance.

Not only does the neglect by Amenhetep III of his imperial responsibilities provide just that interlude of weak administration which would have favoured an invasion of Canaan from the east, but no other such opportunity seems to have occurred for many years afterwards. From the time when Thothmes III definitely established the suzerainty of Egypt over Canaan by the capture of no fewer than 113 of its cities, beginning with the sack of Megiddo about 1478 B.C., each successive Pharaoh until Amenhetep III is shown by the records to have kept his hand firmly upon the country. After the death of Akhenaton, in whose reign the collapse of the Empire became complete, the authority of the Pharaohs was immediately and vigorously re-established by his three successors; and following these Seti I (1314-1305 B.C.) is known to have suppressed revolts in southern Canaan and the Jordan valley itself, while his successor Rameses II (the Great, 1292-1225 B.C.) raised the prestige of Egypt to a height which it had not known since Thothmes III. It is in fact quite clear from the Egyptian records that we cannot place the successful invasion of Canaan by Joshua in any part of this second period: and it is therefore all the more significant that the name of Israel is to be found on a monument of Rameses' successor Merneptah (c. 1220 B.C.). This inscription reads as follows:

> Plundered is the Canaan with every evil
> Carried off is Askelon,
> Seized upon is Gezer
> Yenoam is made as a non-existent thing
> Israel is desolated, her seed is not
> South Palestine (Kharu) has become a (defenceless) widow.

Not only does this inscription tell us that the Israelites were by this time recognized as an established element in the population of the country, in contrast to their former nomadic state ; but it enables us by elimination to fix the approximate position of their name-seat. All the place names mentioned in this inscription are well known. Canaan refers in general, as has been noticed already (p. 24), to the northern area of which Hazor was the focus, and it included all Galilee and Esdraelon. Askalon and Gezer represent the coast of Philistia. Yenoam was a strategic centre in the north-east, and from its context in other references can be located satisfactorily where the " Way of the Sea " from Acre crossed the Jordan between Beisan and the Lake of Galilee. " Kharu " refers, as translated, to the southern highlands. Thus most of Palestine is represented, and the map will be filled if we assign " Israel " to the position in which it appears in this context between Yenoam and Kharu, that is the northern highlands around and to the south of Shechem. But this is precisely where Joshua is said in the Bible to have established the headquarters of the tribes of Israel after he had made good his footing in the country (Joshua xxiv, 1). After Joshua's death Shechem no longer appears as the chief centre of Israel in Biblical tradition, and it appears from the so-called Blessing of Jacob to have fallen to the Egyptian army before the expansion of Manasseh, while the " House of Joseph ", of which it was the natural centre, was still united :

"Joseph is a fruitful bough
A fruitful bough by the fountain
His branches run over the wall
The archers have sorely grieved him
And shot at him, and persecuted him
But his bow abode in strength."

The specific mention of archers in this extract strongly suggests the Egyptian army, in which the bowmen constituted the main strength of the infantry, as may be seen upon numerous

FIG. 22.
The Pharaoh as an Archer : from a Scarab.

monuments and in models. A representation of the Pharaoh as an archer was actually found at Jericho and is here reproduced (Fig. 22).

This interesting aspect of our enquiry could easily be pursued further, but it might lead us from the point we are discussing. Enough has been said to demonstrate the harmony of Israelite tradition at this stage with contemporary Egyptian records[1]; and bearing in mind the archæological

[1] Further points of correspondence between the chronology of Imperial Egypt and that of the Bible history, based upon the date established for the fall of Jericho, will be found set out in a chart at the end of this chapter.

evidence of the site, in which the series of Royal Scarabs is a decisive feature, we find it impossible to place the episode of the Fall of Jericho elsewhere than in the interlude of military inactivity on the part of Amenhetep III.

THE RUINS UNDER A CURSE. There is, however, one further piece of evidence which may be said to amount to final proof. In the Book of Joshua (vi, 26) we are told that the ruins of Jericho were placed under a curse:

> "*And Joshua charged them with an oath at that time saying, Cursed be the man before the Lord that riseth up and buildeth this city Jericho.*"

Though there are signs of partial or occasional occupation of the site, the fact remains that the city itself was left in ruins for five hundred years after its destruction. To make this quite clear we may briefly review the evidence which has already to some extent been indicated.

One group of small dwellings arose in the 13th Century B.C., or perhaps a little earlier, against the parapet of the northern rampart of the Third City: those we examined might have housed four or five families, but there may have been others which had been previously dug away. Relics of this period include a late and rather dull sub-Mycenæan pot found above the destruction layer of the Fourth City at the far side of the outer fosse (which had long before been filled up); and possibly also the small group of vessels, already mentioned, found in the separate top layer of a re-used tomb (No. 13) in the necropolis. These are illustrated for completeness of this record in Fig. 21. Their significance has already been discussed, but it should be noted that no such specimens have been found within the area of the historic city.

More important and more durable was a sort of block-house, built solidly of stone, probably towards the end of the same century or maybe in the reign of Rameses III (1198-1167 B.C.). This occupied the point of vantage near the spring where it covered the remains of the royal residence of the Fourth City, a fact which in itself gives proof of a considerable interval in the local occupation of the site. The section reproduced in Fig. 3 illustrates this point. The rooms of this building had been cleared before we began excavations there, so that the evidence as to its precise date was not definite. But the fragments recovered, together with some notes supplied by the former excavator, gave fairly reliable indications of an Early Iron Age building. Its plan may be seen in Fig. 4, the uppermost building of the series. When we take into account also the great strength of its walls and the curious arrangement of the rooms, we can hardly deem it suitable for a private residence, though it would serve admirably for a military outpost or block-house. This explanation gains some support from the fact that about the same time the old cremation pit (mentioned on p. 116) came again into use, indicating as before the presence of a limited number of people with foreign burial practices. This intrusive element strongly suggests a garrison of foreign mercenaries, for the Egyptians were still masters of the country and are known to have stationed military posts at various strategic centres, for instance at Beisan. Whether in this case it comprised Sherdens as was usual, or Philistines, or some other unit of their foreign troops, is not clear from the material evidence. This included a scarab of this (" Rames-

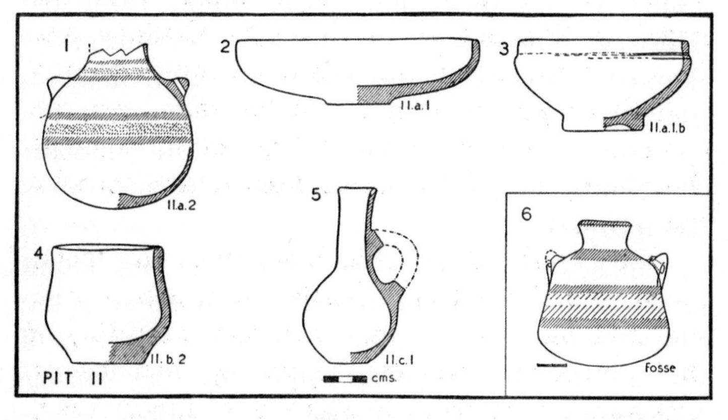

FIG. 23.
Later pottery found outside the limits of the City.

side ") period, engraved with the representation of a foreign deity standing upon an animal's back (Fig. 19), and also a number of large bracelets both of iron and of bronze, in about equal proportions, as well as a group of vessels which seem to be local products belonging also to this period of transition. From Egyptian sources we know that during this reign Philistines were established in the coastal plain, and from the Bible we gather that they were ultimately entrusted with the maintenance of order, at any rate in the south, and that they gradually assumed control, for

At that Time the Philistines had Rule over Israel.

It is thus possible that the block-house in question upon the old mound at Jericho was occupied by a garrison of Philistines under Rameses III to watch and defend the fords of Jordan; while its inception may have dated from the reign of Rameses II in the 13th Century B.C. For completeness of this record we must mention that there may be assigned to the same Age the contents of a small pottery kiln found amongst the tombs, one of which had been cleared out for the purpose.

THE FIFTH CITY. We have thus not found much to indicate even a partial occupation of the site after the city was destroyed, and a scrutiny of the admirably complete report by the former excavators, who worked over these upper levels, does little to fill the gap; the period from 1100 to 900 B.C. is in fact hardly represented at all. About 900 B.C., however, when the second phase of the Iron Age was dawning, there is a sudden and obvious recrudescence of activity. Upon the mound itself there still remain traces of lime revetments or *pisé* work by which the neglected slopes were now consolidated; and in one or two of the highest spots, notably upon the "migdol" or citadel, some brick masonry seemingly belonged to the new city wall, though it may possibly represent a reconstruction of the tower at the later period of the Maccabees as mentioned by Josephus. The previous excavators found plentiful evidence of the later Iron Age culture. The Fifth City would thus represent the Jericho associated in Bible history with the visit of Elijah, and it would

FIG. 24.
Early Iron Age Pottery of City V : c. 800 B.C.

be here that Elisha was saluted as his successor by the Sons of the Prophets who dwelt in the neighbourhood.

Looking back, we find that the four questions we set out to examine have been fully and harmoniously answered. We have compared our archæological results with the indications of the Bible narrative, both as regards the features of the Fourth City as well as the manner and date of its destruction ; and we also have tested the implied setting of the narrative in the scheme of Egyptian history based upon that date, without finding any radical discrepancy. On the contrary much of the detail convinces us not only that the fall of the Fourth City is that described in the Book of Joshua, but that the narrative embodies the tradition of an eye-witness. Finally we have seen that for five hundred years the local occupation remained partial and intermittent ; and though the history of the Fifth City itself is obscure, we find no reason to doubt the validity of the Biblical tradition, narrated in I Kings, xvi, 34, to the effect that in the days of Ahab (876 B.C.) Hiel the Bethelite rebuilt Jericho, upon the long deserted site of the historic City.

Table showing the accordance of the traditional chronological outline of Israel under Joshua and the Judges with the known course of Egyptian activities in Canaan: based upon c. 1390 B.C. for the Fall of Jericho.

x denotes periods of war in Canaan.
o denotes periods of Oppression for Israel.

The continuous vertical lines indicate the periods of effective Egyptian rule (L) and consequent Peace for Israel (R).

EGYPT AND CANAAN.	B.C.	TRADITIONAL CHRONOLOGY OF ISRAEL.
Reign of Thothmes III.		The oppression in Egypt.
	1450	
Amenhetep II. . . 1447		1445, The Exodus under Moses.
Thothmes IV . . 1420		Desert wanderings.
Amenhetep III . . 1411		
	1400	
Decline of Prestige.		Joshua becomes leader. JERICHO (CITY IV) DESTROYED.
Habiru inroads.		Hazor burnt.
		Joshua at Shechem.
Akhenaton . . 1375		
Canaan in disorder		The Elders.
Sakere 1358		
Tutankhamon . . 1356		
Harmhab . . 1350	1350	
EGYPTIAN RULE RE-ESTABLISHED		Forty years "Rest".
Seti I 1314		
Nine years Wars, extending to Trans-Jordan.		Oppression by Eglon of Moab for eighteen years.
	1300	
Rameses II . . 1292		
LONG PERIOD OF EFFECTIVE IMPERIAL RULE.		EIGHTY YEARS OF "REST" FOR ISRAEL.
	1250	

Egypt and Canaan		B.C.		Traditional Chronology of Israel
[Ben Anath, an Egyptian sea captain.]		1250		[Shamgar Ben Anath saves Israel.]
Merneptah .. 1225	x		o	Shechem no more headquarters of Israel.
Israel desolated 1220	x		o	
	x		o	
Usurper and Anarchy	x		o	Oppression by Sisera for Twenty Years.
	x		o	
	x		o	
	x		o	Deborah and Barak rally the tribes.
	x		o	
	x		o	
Setnekht		1200		
Rameses III .. 1198				
Mercenary Garrisons				Forty Years " Rest."
Rameses IV .. 1167 Sinai evacuated				
			o	Midianite oppression 9 years.
			o	
			o	1154 Gideon made king.
		1150		
Decline of Egyptian Authority.				Forty Years " Rest " under Israel's Own King.
Rameses XI .. 1118				
Egypt withdraws from Syria.		1100		Philistine oppression (Samson.)

CHAPTER VIII

JERICHO AND THE EXODUS

(J. B. E. G.)

CHAPTER VIII

I

Lord, when thou wentest out of Seir,
When thou marchedst out of the field of Edom,
The earth trembled, and the heavens dropped,
The clouds also dropped water.

(The Song of Deborah).

NOW that we have discussed each aspect of the Fall of Jericho, and determined the approximate place of that episode within the framework of Egyptian history, we are in a position to examine the wider background in the Bible narrative.

We are of course concerned chiefly with the entry of the Israelites into Canaan ; but in order to appreciate fully this climax to their wanderings we must go back to the time of their departure from Egypt. For a consideration of the story of the Exodus will not only give reliance to the above description of Jericho's destruction ; it will explain the confidence, triumph, and faith that the Israelites felt in Jehovah's powers, when he unlocked for them the barred gateway into the Promised Land. At Jericho two worlds meet, the world which lives for us still in the imperishable records of the Old Testament, and the world of modern scientific research which lifts it out of the darkness of semi-legend and sets it in the full light of history. But at Jericho we are witnessing only the *finale* of that amazing story which began a generation earlier. What was it that really happened when "Israel came out of Egypt?" We may find ourselves in a position now to answer this question, and certainly we cannot regard our task as ended till we have at least made the attempt.

The most lasting impression we receive from reading the story of the Exodus is that of miraculous grandeur.[1] To the Israelites, who since the days of the "Pharaoh which knew not Joseph" had suffered extreme hardship at the hands of their Egyptian taskmasters, their escape from such servitude naturally seemed miraculous and awe-inspiring. But the most extraordinary feature of this story is the vividness with which it was handed down from generation to generation. The prophets and the psalmists, who wrote about seven hundred years after the events, are full of allusions to this great deliverance from Egypt; they quote it to illustrate the Power and Might of Jehovah, and to emphasize the favoured position and religious call of Israel.

Events such as these, which could exert such profound influence on the lives and beliefs of succeeding generations, could not have been ordinary in any sense; and interpretations that

[1] The writer acknowledges his indebtedness in this study of the Exodus to the inspiring book of Canon W. J. Phythian-Adams, *The Call of Israel* (Oxford University Press).

try to " explain away " the miraculous nature of the happenings are not convincing. For instance, would the Israelites have been impressed by the " plague of darkness " if it were merely (as some suggest) a violent sandstorm ? Would the " pillar of cloud by day and the pillar of fire by night " have inspired generations of story tellers, if it were merely a brazier filled with burning wood such as is often borne along at the head of a caravan of pilgrims or an army ? Would writers seven hundred years later have told of the crossing of the Red Sea as the crowning miracle of this deliverance, the greatest example of Jehovah's power and protection, if, as one of them suggests, the waters had been merely blown to one side down the beach by a strong wind ?

No. It is clear that these events were great beyond the understanding of those who witnessed them. The Israelites, with fear clutching at their hearts, despairing of all hope of life, let alone freedom, were confronted by such a series of miraculous happenings that not only was safety assured but escape became easy. Their religion and their literature point to no other conclusion.

What then was so miraculous that it effected the escape of the Israelites, and so great that the vivid impression it created was never effaced ? If what the Israelites considered " miraculous " was really a natural phenomenon beyond the reach of their understanding, then we do know of one possible explanation that would satisfy all the stories of the Exodus. Briefly it is suggested that the miraculous phenomenon which facilitated the Exodus was nothing more nor less than a violent and widely-extended volcanic upheaval. Let it be said at the outset that there is no direct proof that this interpretation is correct ; but the reader will probably agree that even a fraction of the circumstantial evidence available would point to that conclusion.

Frequent reference has already been made to the volcanic rift in which Jericho was situated. Now this is but the northern end of a well-known geological fault which can be traced—staggering as the distance may seem—for fully four thousand miles. Its course from North to South can be followed along the line of the Jordan Valley and its continuation the Arabah, through the Red Sea (where it is marked by numerous volcanic islands), into the heart of Central Africa, where it is met by a similar rift descending from the North and enclosing with it the sources of the Nile. The importance of this feature for our present enquiry lies in the fact observed by modern scientists that there is a real physical connexion along the whole length of any geological fault ; so that earthquakes and volcanic eruptions at one end could herald similar disturbances at the other, and in fact during the cycle of years when such disturbances are recorded no single part of its whole length could be considered as immune.

Now it is suggested that at the time of the Exodus (about 1450 B.C.) the whole of this geological two-fold rift from Palestine to Lake Nyasa was in a state of violent seismic and volcanic upheaval, and that it is this which explains the apparently supernatural phenomena which facilitated Israel's escape from Egypt and brought them finally to the walls of Jericho. Let us then take these phenomena in order and see what light this theory throws upon them.

First the " plagues ". One of the most common results of volcanic disturbances is the muddy poisonous matter that is discharged from craters and cracks in the earth. To quote a tragic example, as a result of the eruption of Mont Pelée in 1902, all the streams on one side of the island were turned into muddy cataracts of black and poisonous water. Great quantities of dead fish were later observed floating at the mouths of these rivers, whence came an overpowering smell of sulphur. Is it not likely that those far-distant sources of the Nile were affected in the same way? If the reader will only glance at Exodus vii to x, he will see at once that this interpretation not only explains the series of " miraculous " plagues, but is the only one to do so. " The waters that were in the river were turned into blood. And the fish that was in the river died ; and the river stank, and the Egyptians could not drink of the water of the river." This description could not be bettered, in its careful recording of the unpleasant facts, by the most matter-of-fact modern scientist. It explains, too, why " the frogs came up " in swarms out of the poisoned river, only to die in their turn so that

" the land stank " with their corrupting carcasses. A plague of flies (in the most literal sense) naturally followed, and so began that widespread pestilence which fell alike on man and beast.

Meantime, while the lakes at the sources of the Nile were belching forth their poison, violent disturbances may be assumed to have been taking place in the north-eastern section of the rift. To the east of the Red Sea, in the land of Midian, a volcano was in eruption—Mount Horeb, " the Mount of God ". Those who have been present at volcanic eruptions testify to the clouds of dark ash that are often emitted : during the eruption of Vesuvius in 1906 an impenetrable pall of darkness covered Naples and the surrounding country ; and after the eruption of Tomboro (East Indies) in 1815 there was darkness for three days at a distance of three hundred miles. Where else should we look for the explanation of the " plague of darkness ", a " darkness that could be felt ", and of the thunderstorms and torrential rain and hail that are so characteristic of volcanic disturbances ? " And Moses stretched forth his rod toward heaven : and the Lord sent thunder and hail, and the fire ran along upon the ground ; and the Lord rained hail upon the land of Egypt."

" The pillar of cloud by day and the pillar of fire by night " can now also be visualised as it really was—a column of dust and steam and ash from the open mouth of an active volcano. Nothing else will account for the vividness of this guiding light of safety as it appeared to the Israelites, who had such faith in this " miraculous " sign that they followed it blindly out of the land of their captivity.

And where did it lead them? At first to the north end of the Red Sea, where their way was barred by the water on their right, and the Egyptian frontier-posts on their left. While this nomad host stood there trembling and despairing, at the Scylla and Charybdis of its flight, the waters suddenly " went back " and the sea was " made dry land ", so that " the children of Israel went into the midst of the sea upon dry ground ". Only a great recession of the sea, such as frequently occurs during earthquake disturbances before a tidal wave, could account for the wonder of this story, and the place it held in the minds of future generations. When the waters returned, and the tidal wave destroyed the pursuing Egyptians, " covering their chariots, and the horsemen, and all the host of Pharaoh that came into the sea after them ", well might the Israelites receive an ineradicable impression of their God's almighty greatness.

But that was not all. A further example of His majesty was made manifest when the Israelites stood at the foot of the " Mount of God ". And who can read the narrative (Exodus xix, 16-19) without realizing that it describes perfectly the terrific convulsions of a volcano? " And it came to pass on the third day in the morning, that there were thunders and lightnings, and a thick cloud upon the mount, and the voice of the trumpet exceeding loud ; so that all the people that was in the camp trembled. . . . And Mount Sinai was altogether on a smoke, because the Lord descended upon it in fire : and the smoke thereof ascended as the smoke of a furnace, and the whole mount quaked greatly. And when the voice of the trumpet sounded long, and waxed louder and louder, Moses spake, and God answered him by a voice ". So Israel learned through outward signs and wonders the " consuming fire " of Him who had called them.

This modern interpretation of the story of the Exodus relies on circumstantial evidence, but the verdict can only be in its favour. Never did physical facts so plainly illustrate the origins of an ancestral memory. Even though the story has been embellished by later writers who wished either to exaggerate its miracles or to give a rational explanation of the events as they conceived them—the substance of it is seen on this interpretation to rest upon a solid core of fact. It affords, in short, not merely a proof of the accuracy of Israel's tradition, but a reason for that faith which survived so many shocks of fortune.

On this latter point, however, there is something more to be said. It must not be thought that, just because the story has been explained, it therefore necessarily ceases to be miraculous. Was it not miraculous, from a believing man's point of view, that God should so order the phenomena of nature in a way that suited His will ? He wished to save and inspire His Chosen People, and here was everything ready for His purpose. If the means employed were miraculous in the eyes of the Israelites—then God's wish was fulfilled. There was no need for " miracles " in the old sense of the word when great forces from the bowels of the earth lay at His disposal.

We may now move onwards with Israel from Horeb to the frontiers of the Promised Land. As it is the main purpose of this enquiry to consider the part played by seismic phenomena in the departure of the Israelites from Egypt in so far as they throw light on their entry into Canaan, we are not concerned to any great extent with their " forty years " of wanderings ; though it would not be irrelevant for the same reason to refer in passing to the story of Korah, Dathan and Abiram, who at some point in these wanderings (Numbers xvi, 27-35) led a rebellion against Moses, and were destroyed when " the ground clave asunder that was under them : And the earth opened her mouth, and swallowed them up . . . So they, and all that appertained to them, went down alive into the pit : and the earth closed upon them."

Such incidents in the Bible narrative, considered singly, could never sway our judgment and lead us to any particular conclusion. It is only when we consider them in conjunction with others—as in this case with the stories of the destruction of Sodom and Gomorrah (Genesis xix, 24-25), of Moses striking the rock (Numbers xx, 2-11), of Elijah's mysterious end (2 Kings ii, 1-12)—that the reiterated evidence begins to point to a conclusion in no undecided manner. For it is possible that these isolated episodes, together with allusions such as the quotation at the head of this chapter and the opening verses of Psalm 114, all point to recurring seismic activity in the Jordan Rift, and that they are in fact founded on well-observed but ill-understood happenings such as those experienced by the Israelites during their escape from Egypt.

But, as has been said, our present enquiry is concerned not so much with the desert wanderings of the Israelites as with the events that marked their conclusion ; and as much depends on a true appreciation of their nature and importance if we are to gain any real understanding of Old Testament history, we should first try to recapture the setting, to picture once more the actual scene, as far as it can be reconstructed from the results of the excavations on the spot.

2

" *And Joshua the son of Nun sent out of Shittim two men to spy secretly, saying, Go view the land, even Jericho.*" (Joshua ii, 1.)

Across the Jordan Valley, at the foot of the hills of Moab, the Israelites had pitched their camp at Abel Shittim, and from there they could look almost due westwards to Jericho. Eagerly they must have gazed towards the borders of the Promised Land, and the first visible example of the " cities fenced and strong " of which they had heard such discouraging reports. A watcher on the neighbouring mound of Kufren could look far up and down the Jordan Valley ; to his right it stretched northwards till the heat-haze closed the view ; to his left lay the deceptively beautiful waters of the Dead Sea ; to the north and south alike the valley was bounded by the ridge of the Judæan plateau, rose-red in the sunshine, scored with the shadows of dry torrent-beds. Up one or other of those savage ravines their way would lie into the " land flowing with milk and honey "; no easy ascent for the slow-moving host, hampered with flocks and herds, women and children and baggage-animals. Almost straight opposite Jebel Kuruntul stood out conspicuous from the mountain-ridge, and at its foot, enfolded in its shadow as afternoon crept on, lay Jericho upon its mound, the first man-made obstacle to the Promised Land.

The towered city, dimly visible, gave no sign ; but it was obvious that once the Jordan was crossed such a position could not be left unmastered, to threaten the line of their further march. So the spies were sent out to measure the strength of this first enemy, and mingling, we may suppose, with other travellers whose arrival would cause no comment, they penetrated unnoticed into the city.

We may picture them as they plodded in the heat across the plains, looking at the mound and the thick walls crowning the summit. Their goal must have been the eastern gate above the spring, beside the ancient tower, over which ran the newer fortifications. With a guard of the King's armed men at the entrance, it must have appeared very impressive to the spies, accustomed as they were to the tent life of the desert.

The eastern gate-tower with the adjoining Palace, though perhaps the most imposing feature to anyone approaching the high walls from the plain, did not actually occupy the highest part of the mound. The western edge stood somewhat higher, so that behind the Palace the buildings of the interior rose in *échelon*, culminating in the lofty north-west angle-tower. The great size and better preservation of this tower led us to believe at first that it might be the citadel of Jericho, but the progress of excavation revealed the trace of three other mural towers ; that in the south-west was particularly strong, and must have played an important part in the main line of defence.

Once past the gate, the spies were within a very small, cramped town ; its whole area, five acres, must have been very crowded with people and animals from the fields. As in all such ancient towns, its flat-roofed houses were huddled irregularly along narrow streets, little more than alleys, and inadequately paved or drained. They had even been allowed to encroach upon the walls and the space between, which in parts was bridged by timbers or crossed by narrow bonding-walls that served as a foundation. As this space was some fifteen feet at most, these dwellings must have been small and slight, perched precariously over a sort of tunnel running round the city, and reached presumably by walking along the walls from certain points that were accessible or over the neighbours' roofs as is not uncommon in hill-side villages of the Near East to-day. The military drawbacks of such a cumbering of the fortifications were obvious, but apparently disregarded. The view across the city from one of the angle-towers must have been very like that still to be seen in the mediæval quarters of many old continental towns, piled at varying heights about the cathedral or some other large building.

The houses in Jericho were built of mud-brick, containing but few rooms. Some were thatched with palm leaves or reeds from the Jordan fens, for charred remains of such roofing material were found, fallen upon the floors below. The living-room served as kitchen and store-room alike; the blackened cooking-pot stood on the fire in one corner, the pottery grain-bin in another. Wheat, barley and oats were all in use, and the flour was baked into rough cakes of bread. Dates and olives, onions and peppercorns, figured among the simple family provisions. The general impression we receive from discoveries in this Fourth City is one of simplicity and relative poverty.

Such was Jericho at the time of the spies' visit; and they must have been greatly heartened by what they saw and heard. Not only was the city small, but the inhabitants, who knew well about the coming of the Israelites, were dreading their further advance. The isolated position of Jericho was never better illustrated than during this critical period of her history. The Israelites, whose escape from Egypt forty years before had been accompanied by such disastrous experiences for the Egyptians, were now reported to be approaching Canaan; yet the representative of Egypt—still the ruling power—who lived at Jerusalem a bare twenty miles away, did not raise a finger to help Jericho. Well might the people be afraid; they of the Jordan Valley had never been warriors, and they knew that their only hope of defence lay in the double line of their walls. Rahab probably summed up their feelings accurately enough when she said: "Your terror is fallen upon us, and all the inhabitants of the land faint because of you." (Joshua ii, 9.)

The story of her pact with the spies is too well-known to need quoting in full here: its chief interest for us lies in its disclosure that she lived in one of those houses on the wall. She "let them down by a cord through the window; for her house was upon the town wall, and she dwelt upon the wall". From there, following her advice, the men fled to the lofty mountain on the west of Jericho, whence, having baffled their pursuers, they returned across the Jordan.

The crossing of the Jordan by the Israelites themselves was the next stage in their advance. "And it came to pass, when the people removed from their tents, to pass over Jordan, the priests bearing the ark of the covenant before the people; and as they that bare the ark were come unto Jordan, and the feet of the priests that bare the ark were dipped in the brim of the water (for Jordan overfloweth all his banks all the time of harvest), that the waters which came down from above stood and rose up upon an heap, very far from the city Adam, that is beside Zaretan: and those that came down toward the sea of the plain, even the Salt Sea, failed, and were cut off: and the people passed over right against Jericho. And the priests that bare the ark of the covenant of the Lord stood firm on dry ground in the midst of Jordan, and all the Israelites passed over on dry ground, until all the people were passed clean over Jordan." (Joshua iii, 14-17.)

Of this miraculous drying-up of the river-bed something has already been said in a previous chapter. We saw reason to believe then that it was probably due to an earthquake, and we can now place it with confidence in the context of the other miraculous phenomena of the Exodus. The story of Dathan and Abiram to which reference was made a few pages back suggests that the convulsions in the Jordan Rift had as yet by no means subsided. Moreover the nature of the destruction of Jericho itself, as suggested by discoveries on the site, points to the same conclusion; and it only remains to consider the graphic details of its last days in the words of the Old Testament.

Now Jericho was straitly shut up because of the children of Israel: none went out, and none came in.

And the Lord said unto Joshua, See, I have given into thine hand Jericho, and the king thereof, and the mighty men of valour.

There is no difficulty now in understanding the note of confident faith which breathes in every line of the Bible narrative (Joshua vi). For the writer, recounting the events long afterwards, this was the only mood in which he could imagine the people advancing. They had been helped, at every stage of their escape from Egypt, by the timely manifestations of Jehovah's power—surely He would not fail them now ? Had He not brought plagues on the Egyptians ? Had He not driven back the waters of the Red Sea—and later the waters of the Jordan—at the one and only moment when this would mean everything to the hopes of Israel ? Surely now He would help them to overpower this city, the sacrifice of which would seal His covenant with the Chosen People ?

Such must indeed have been the feelings, if not of the common people, at least of their leader ; and the narrative, though we cannot perhaps trust all its details, seems to reflect clearly his unshakable faith in the Divine assistance. Certainly no other siege has ever been conducted like this one, the awful and dramatic tenseness of which never fails to thrill the reader. First of all the Israelite warriors were ordered to stand in a circle round the city : "And ye shall compass (i.e. encircle) the city, all ye men of war, and go about the city once. Thus shalt thou do six days."

Then came a daily religious procession: "The seven priests bearing the seven trumpets of rams' horns passed on before the Lord, and blew with the trumpets: and the ark of the covenant of the Lord followed them." And all this took place in an ominous silence: "Ye shall not shout, nor make any noise with your voice, neither shall any word proceed out of your mouth, until the day I bid you shout; then shall ye shout." The circle of watchful men, and the solemn procession—these would bring fear to the heart of any besieged city. But when in addition to this one tries to imagine the silence—and there was silence for six days, broken only by notes from the "trumpets of rams' horns"—then one can feel all the horror of anticipation that must have been felt by the inhabitants of Jericho.

> "*And it came to pass on the seventh day, that they rose early about the dawning of the day, and compassed the city after the same manner seven times.*"

What happened on that fateful day? We cannot know for certain—but, if we feel any confidence in our interpretation of the stories of the Exodus, we can picture the scene and know in our hearts that our picture is correct. For what reader, who has assented to the theory advanced in this chapter, will suppose that the walls of Jericho fell by the hand of man? Only the miracle of an earthquake shock will justify the description of this event in the Book of Joshua.

Here again we cannot but sense that note of

confidence, the sure expectation that this was the day on which Jehovah would manifest His Power once more : it was " only on that day " that they " compassed the city seven times ". The shout raised by the Israelites at Joshua's command, often assumed (according to certain interpretations of the Bible narrative) to be the cause of the walls' destruction, was no doubt raised because they no less than their leader sensed the imminence of that supreme disaster. While these nomad people were encircling the city, with no proper military equipment, let alone siege engines and implements, they must have realized to the full their own helplessness, and their inability to capture such a city unaided ; yet as they stood there waiting they became conscious of something—something they seemed to recognize—yes, something surely that had helped them before. " The earth trembled " —and suddenly they realized, with the highest feelings of exultation, that this was the way in which Jericho would be destroyed ; that the Power who had driven back the waters of the Red Sea, who had spoken to them from the Mount of God, and had stemmed the flow of the river Jordan, would now destroy the walls of Jericho before their eyes.

And when the priests blew with the trumpets, Joshua said unto the people, Shout ; for the Lord hath given you the city. . . . So the people shouted, and the priests blew with the trumpets : and it came to pass, when the people heard the sound of the trumpet, that the people shouted with a great shout, and the wall fell down flat, so that the people went up into the city, every man straight before him, and they took the city. (Joshua vi, 16-20.)

Now was the moment for Jehovah's sacrifice. When the walls crashed down the slope, dragging in their ruin the houses they had supported, then the besiegers went up, " every man straight before him ", and the work of destruction began. "And they utterly destroyed all that was in the city, both man and woman, young and old, and ox, and sheep, and ass, with the edge of the sword." The people of Jericho, terrified by the silent ritual of the last seven days, and the shock that had destroyed their walls, and the triumphant shout of the invaders whose purpose was now obvious, must have submitted to their doom with helpless fatalism.

And they burnt the city with fire, and all that was therein.

The destruction of Jericho was indeed an act unsurpassed in history, not so much for its frightfulness, as for the firm deliberation with which it was accomplished. Ever and again the desert areas of the Near East have given birth to holy wars. The first flood of the Mohammedan invaders, the fiery Mahdists of two generations ago, the stern fanatical Wahabis of to-day, all stained their trails with blood in the name of their religion. But there is no record of a determination comparable with this, the solemn sacrifice of an entire town. The annihilation of Jericho was no ordinary incident of raid, but the first step in the fulfilment of the Covenant. Nor was the slaying of its population a mere case of blood-lust ; just as the firstborn of each family of Israel was dedicated to their God, and the firstlings of the flocks were sacrificed, so Jericho, as the first-fruits of the Promised Land, was devoted in its entirety to Jehovah. There were no spoils and no captives. Only the woman who had helped the Israelites' cause was saved with her family ; all others were doomed to be sacrificed within the city in one awful holocaust.

Over the smouldering ruins of this vast and dreadful burnt-offering, or perhaps while lighting the sacrificial fire, Joshua pronounced the solemn curse of the Lord upon the man who should rise up and build this city Jericho ; and after five thousand years and more of busy life upon the spot, the mound was left silent and desolate at last.

THE END

APPENDICES

TABLE SHOWING THE RELATION OF CONTEMPORARY PERIODS AND

Date. B.C.	Culture Period.		Characteristics.
			STONE
Before 5000	Middle Stone Age or Mesolithic Period [Unconfirmed].		Microlithic flints. Two metre deposit below the Neolithic levels. ? rock shelters.
	LATE STONE AGE		
4500	Lower Neolithic Period	i.	No pottery: flint industry includes Tahunian types. Developed architectural features: burnished floors and walls: *Megaron*-like Temple. Figurines of domesticated animals, and fertility emblems.
4000	Middle Neolithic Period.	ii.	Invention of pottery; flint industry and architectural features continuing. Earliest statuary.
3500	Upper Neolithic (? Chalcolithic) Period.	iii.	Pottery finished on slow hand-wheel: developed shapes, painting restricted, incised ornament. Distinctive flint industry (Jerichoan), derived from the preceding period. Hard house floors. Grain silos.

THE SUCCESSIVE CITIES OF JERICHO TO
EPISODES WITH DATES IN ROUND FIGURES.

Biblical Episodes, etc.	*External Synchronisms.*
AGE	
	(Mesolithic caves on Mt. Carmel).
	Contemporary with the Proto-Chalcolithic (or post-Neolithic) Period at Mersin in S. Asia Minor.
Traditional dispersal of the Sons of Noah from Mt. Ararat: the Semites associated with Arphaxad (Genesis xi).	Contemporary with the Early Chalcolithic Period in N. Mesopotamia (Tell Halaf Culture).
	Distant cultural affinities with Tepe Gawra, near Nineveh, also with Ras Shamra (V) and Judeideh (XIV) in N. Syria, and with the Fayoum (Egypt).
Earliest settlement at Beisan, the Biblical Bethshan.	Contemporary with the Later Chalcolithic Period in S. Mesopotamia (El Ubaid and, towards the end, the Jemdat Nasr cultures) visible in N. Syria at Judeideh (XIII), and in S. Asia Minor at Mersin (XIII-XIV). Possible contacts with Ghassoul (III-IV), Beisan (XVIII), Wady Ghazeh, and Ras Shamra.

CHRONOLOGICAL CHART

BRONZE

Date. B.C.	*Culture Period.*	*City.*	*Characteristics.*
	EARLY BRONZE AGE.		
3000	Early Bronze Age I	I.	Walled city on the mound and northern slope. Rounded buildings giving place to rectangular houses. No bronze objects. Pottery finished on wheel: some linear decoration.
2500	Early Bronze Age II	II.	City rebuilt on top of the mound and protected by great brick walls around the brink. Fortified gateway near the spring. Communal "Tomb A". Increased cultivation of cereals and fruits; extending trade relations.
2000	Middle Bronze Age I.	[No City]	Pottery of a special kind.
1900	Middle Bronze Age II.	III.	*a* Expansion of the city. Stone glacis with fosse and parapet encircles the foot of the mound.
1750	M. B. A. III.	III.	*b* Jericho a Hyksos military outpost and store: Official seals: Bronze weapons. Elegant wheel-made pottery, mostly plain. Period of greatest extension and prosperity.
1600		III.	City totally destroyed.

CHRONOLOGICAL CHART

Biblical Episodes, etc.	*External Synchronisms.*
AGE.	
Foundation of great Biblical cities such as Jerusalem, Shechem, and Megiddo.	Predynastic Egyptian objects below foundations of First City. Babylonian art and religious influence dominant. Early Dynastic Period in S. Babylonia.
	Babylonian and Mesopotamian influences still predominant. Sargon, founder of the First Dynasty of Akkad, extends his Empire to the Mediterranean. Pyramid Age (Old Empire) in Egypt.
The Abrahamic tribes move towards Canaan. (Genesis xii.)	Mari, on the Euphrates, a Babylonian outpost.
The tribe of Lot enters the Jordan valley. (Genesis xii-xiii.) " Four Kings against Five " (Genesis xiv).	Similar wares found on numerous sites in Palestine and Trans-Jordan.
Early Canaanite Period.	Ammi-ditana : " King of the West ". First Dynasty of Babylon, ended by a Hittite raid. Middle Empire of Egypt : contacts with Syria. Mari tablets.
Patriarchal contact with Egypt (Genesis xxxvii).	Hyksos domination in Egypt and Syria ; Cassite Dynasty in Babylonia.
Patriarchal customs based on social practices (of Arphaxad) as later described in the Nuzi Tablets.	
" There arose a new King over Egypt which knew not Joseph" (Exodus i, 8).	Egyptians drive out the Hyksos and establish the New Empire.

CHRONOLOGICAL CHART

Date. B.C.	Culture Period.	City.	Characteristics.
1575		IV.	*a* Brick walled city crowning the mound. Store-rooms and Hyksos Palace partially restored. Hyksos culture survives in tombs and city.
1480	Late Bronze Age I		Egyptian occupation under Hatshepsut and Thothmes III. Changed culture shows effects of Egyptian Imperial relations.
1450			*b* Brick walled city restored, after earthquake, on a more modest scale. Smaller Palace. Tombs and pottery of period Thothmes III to Amenhetep III.
1400			Incipient change of culture. An earthquake damages the city and brings down the walls; buildings and contents destroyed by a great fire. Last scarabs: reign of Amenhetep III.
1385	Late Bronze Age II	[No City]	Site almost deserted.

CHRONOLOGICAL CHART

Biblical Episodes, etc.	*External Synchronisms.*
Traditional period of the Israelite oppression in Egypt. (Exodus i.)	Jericho's King becomes an Egyptian vassal: Seal of the Pharaoh Ka-mes found at Jericho. Contact with Cyprus.
Semite nomads seek sustenance on the Egyptian border.	Epoch of Ugarit (Ras Shamra) and Alalakh (Atchana) in N. Syria. Egyptian Empire reorganized by Thothmes III "Destroyer of the Hyksos". Nuzi tablets.
Moses (Exodus iii). Exodus of the Israelites and others from Egyptian border provinces (Exodus xiii-xiv). Volcanic phenomena of Horeb (Exodus xix).	Amenhetep III grows old, neglects his Empire, and withdraws his troops.
Joshua. The Jordan dammed at Adam (? Ed Damieh). Capture and total destruction of Jericho (City IV) by the Israelites (Joshua i-vi).	No intervention from Egypt or neighbouring cities of Palestine, where the Habiru inroads are suborning the terrified population.
Ruined city under a curse (Joshua vi, 26). Inroad of Ammon and Amalek under Eglon of Moab (Judges iii, 13).	Pharaoh Seti I represses revolts in South Palestine and Trans-Jordania (1315 B.C.)

CHRONOLOGICAL CHART

Date. B.C.	Culture Period.	City.	Characteristics.
			IRON
1285–1150	Early Iron Age I		Stone Block-house on Spring Hill. Partial occupation of northern slope. Cremation pit: foreign garrison. A few old tombs re-used.
		[No City]	
			Casual occupation of the site.
900	Early Iron Age II.	V.	Brick walled city: slopes reinforced by pisé work. Characteristic pottery. (Excavated by Dr. Watzinger.)
720			[Probable fall of Jericho.]

CHRONOLOGICAL CHART

Biblical Episodes, etc.	*External Synchronisms.*
AGE.	
Long period of " rest " under the	effective suzerainty of Rameses II (1292-1225).
"The Archers have sorely grieved him and shot at him " (Genesis xlix. 23).	Merneptah desolates S. Palestine and mentions Israel (1220 B.C.).
Epic of Sisera and Deborah : c. 1200 B.C.	Inroads of northerners : Philistines established on the southern coast (Rameses III, 1198-1167).
Midianite and Amalekite inroads (Judges vii, 12).	Decline of Egyptian power.
Israel makes Gideon King.	
Philistines rule over Israel (Judges xiv).	
Jericho rebuilt during reign of Ahab (c. 875 B.C.), as recorded in I Kings xvi, 34.	
Jericho visited by Elijah and Elisha (II Kings ii, 1-22).	Assyrian and Babylonian conquests (Sargon, 722 B.C.)
Fall of Samaria.	Revolt of Mesha of Moab.

NOTES ON THE ILLUSTRATIONS

FRONTISPIECE

The Fourth City of Jericho, totally destroyed between 1400 and 1388 B.C. as described in Chapter VII; from a monochrome drawing by Miss Mabel Ratcliffe. Pages 131–132, 166–170.

PLATE I. SOME VIEWS AT JERICHO

a: A general view of the oasis of Jericho from the ancient site, with Elisha's Fountain in the foreground; the pools are relatively modern. The Expedition's house is the extreme right one in the trees. In the background are the Hills of Moab faintly seen and (below) the Dead Sea. Pages 8–9, 30.

b: A view (taken also from the mound) of a neighbouring farm-house in which the main building and outhouses are all continuously roofed. The entrance is supported by wooden posts. Page 47.

c: A view of the lower end of the Wadi Kelt, probably the Valley of Achor, and on the south side a mound of ruins which marks the site of the summer palace of Herod the Great. Page 10.

PLATE II. THE ANCIENT SITE OF JERICHO UNDER EXCAVATION

a: General view of the site from the western foothills with the hills of Moab faintly seen in the background. Between the road and the north end of the mound the white patch indicates the area of the Necropolis. The mound is seen as it was when we arrived there, fissured and disturbed by former excavation and subsequent attrition. Pages 30, 38.

b: Preparing to excavate the north-eastern corner of the City; clearing away a former tip-heap. Page 31.

c: The Professor among the pots, studying the contents of "layer g" in Tomb 5. Pages 26 and 112.

NOTES ON ILLUSTRATIONS

PLATE III. THE POTTERY BENCH (Mrs. J. Garstang) AND TWO REPAIRED VESSELS

a : A vase in the shape of a bird ; Cypriote style ; City IVa. Pages 98 and 112.

b : Probably a libation vase, beautifully made, pinky-red pottery, burnished and painted ; was repaired from 73 fragments. At the divided handle is a moulded snake, the head of which can be seen turning over the handle towards the mouth of the vessel ; City III. Pages 28–29, 97–98.

PLATE IV. THE BEGINNING OF OUR EXCAVATIONS

a : The ruined walls of Jericho around the brink of the main north-western corner, as seen before our work began. The high part of the walls (left) proved to mark the site of the north-western tower or migdol. The main wall in the foreground is the northern wall of City II. Some remains of the outer screen wall are seen on the right. In the background is the Jebel Kuruntul. Pages 78–79, 109–110, 167.

b : The start of the work on the north-western tower or migdol : brick walls coming to light. In the foreground are two French archæologists, one of whom is Professor Moret. Pages 109–110.

c : Work progressing in the north-east corner. House walls against the main rampart of City II and other buildings coming to light. Page 79.

PLATE V. WALL PLANS OF THE FOUR CITIES

This plate shows the successive outlines of the four cities, with some of the excavated buildings of each level. The squares enable the changes of shape to be realized, but the contours vary with the age of each city.

In City II the gate-tower and gateway are a novel feature. In the Third City the outline of the Palace and store-rooms appears on Spring Hill, and in the Fourth is a plan of the last royal residence over the site of the store-rooms, also the migdol in the north-west. The changing position of the spring is note-worthy, starting near the north-eastern angle and gradually moving southward towards where the water now seeps into the pools. These positions are a matter of inference.

First City: 3000 B.C. Second City: 2500 B.C.
Third City: 1900 B.C. Fourth City: 1580 B.C.

Pages 69–70, 78–82, 91–93, 108–111.

PLATE VI. SECTION THROUGH THE EXCAVATED AREA IN THE NORTH-EAST CORNER

Levels I-III. Elevation of Main Wall and houses of City II.

IV-VII Buildings of City I.

VIII-XVII. Neolithic floors and house walls; Earthquake crack and *Megaron*-like temple on Levels XI and XII.

This Section shows the main rampart of City II with its foundations descending at Level III towards the right, and abutting against the rampart the walls of contemporary buildings. In strip 5 are three floor levels of room 100, the wall of which was raised repeatedly throughout the occupation, perhaps even higher than Level I. Buildings below this, in Levels IV to VII, belong to the First City, the outer wall of which is just seen in section in strip 7 at the 5 m. level. Levels IX, X and XI are marked by the continuous Neolithic floors described in the text. Pottery made its appearance in Level IX and Late Neolithic (or Chalcolithic) pottery characterises Level VIII. In the hole which goes down to minus 2 m. are seen successive Neolithic floors below the *megaron* down to Level XVII, and the hollow space below shows where the Microlithic flints were discovered, which indicate possibly a Mesolithic period preceding the Neolithic. Pages 35, 39–64.

PLATE VII. NEOLITHIC FLOORS AND MODEL SHRINE

a: Neolithic floor with temple (left centre), sheep pens, and in the foreground an earthquake fissure running up into a higher level on the right, indicating that the earthquake occurred at a later epoch. In the background (left) is the migdol, and on the right the towering mass of masonry with house walls abutting against it indicates the depth of the Neolithic floors below the walls of

City II. The figure half way down (right) marks the position of the Babylonian shrine of City I. Pages 48–51, 71–72.

b : Model shrine or granary of unbaked marly clay, showing a doorway closed by a rolling stone fitting into a socket; on the left a chamber and above an upper floor, upon which a clay pillar supported the roof, replaced in the photograph by a piece of wood. There were also two windows, one on each side. Height about 3 ft. Pages 56–57.

PLATE VIII. VOTIVE FIGURINES OF ANIMALS: AND NEOLITHIC FLINT IMPLEMENTS

a : Votive figurines found between the *megaron*-like shrine and the sheep-pens, including rams, sheep, goat, ? dog, and (second from the left) a ridged-backed animal which looks like a pig. Pages 49–50, 54.

b : Selected types of Jericho flints and small obsidian tools from the Middle and Lower Neolithic levels. These weapons and implements are classified technically as Tahunian, but as a group they form a distinct series. Nos. 1-6, Arrowheads; 7, 8, Sickle blades; 9-11, Obsidian blades; 12, 13, Obsidian blades. Types from Microlithic Industry: 14, Obsidian blade; 15, 16, Microlithic blades; 17, Retouched Microlith. Pages 49, 52–53.

PLATE IX. THE EARLIEST POTTERY: AND EARTHQUAKE EFFECTS

a : The earliest pots of Jericho, just below (right), and (left) rising above, a laid floor (level IX) of the Neolithic period. Actual position seen on pl. VI at the 7 m. level in strip I (on the left-hand side numbered 452). On the floor below (202) there was no pottery, nor anywhere else on Level X. The right-hand dish or bowl (marked with an arrow) was simply a hollow scooped in the ground through the floor, lined with marl. The bigger pot on the left is more like a grain-bin, descending below floor-level and carried up above it. Pages 54–56.

b : Two interments at level XI, right-hand end of pl. VI, strip 8, number 479. Page 51.

NOTES ON ILLUSTRATIONS

PLATE X. MODELLED HEAD OF THE LATE STONE AGE

Height 8 ins. ; full description in the text, pages 57–58.

PLATE XI. ARCHITECTURAL FEATURES OF CITY I (3000-2500 B.C.)

a : This photograph shows the progress of excavations ; nearing the bottom level of City I, showing the great rampart of City II rising high on the left, its foundation rising steadily towards the left. In course of excavation are the large courtyards of the building divided up with small square rooms and round buildings (? granaries), and just beyond this is the position of the Babylonian shrine (to the left of the work-people) at the floor-level. Pages 69–75.

b : Round granaries and part of an apsidal building (175), crossed by a later wall (left). The steps in the background are work-people's. Pages 74–75.

PLATE XII. GLACIS OF CITY III, AND RAMPARTS OF CITIES II AND IV

a : The Hyksos glaçis descending into the hollow. Behind the figure at the middle level are the remains of the wall of City I, and in front of the upper figure are the remains of the brick parapet built along the top of the glacis. Full description on pages 91–93.

b : Wall of the Fourth City over wall of the Second City. In this case the foundations of IV almost coincide with the line of the bigger wall below. In the latter may be seen weep-holes along the face of the wall ; the bricks are large. The former is seen partly side-view where the boy stands (rather ragged) and mostly in a section cut through it (left). In this the bricks are smaller and a darker colour for the most part ; the foundation stones are visible just below it. This upper wall is the same as the upper wall in Pl. XVIII and the most compact piece of it, probably due to the fact that the foundations were firmly supported at this point, whereas in Pl. XVIII, which is distant about 50 yds. to the south, the foundations overhang the void on the right-hand side. Pages 78–79, 108–111.

NOTES ON ILLUSTRATIONS

PLATE XIII. FINISHED POTTERY STYLES OF HYKSOS PERIOD

a : Some selected pottery vessels of Hyksos period (from Tomb 9); that on the left is decorated with paint; the lower one in the middle is a strainer. Page 99.

b : Plain wares of the same period (restored professionally) illustrating the variety and elegance of the pottery shapes at the time; from a Palace store-room Page 97.

PLATE XIV. HYKSOS RHYTON AND BABYLONIAN BULL'S HEAD

a : Human face on pottery goblet of the Hyksos period (Tomb 9), City III; Pages 100–101.

b : Babylonian Bull's Head carved in darkened ivory; City I. Pages 77–78.

PLATE XV. BRONZES, SCARABS, ETC.; 17th CENTURY, B.C.

A battle axe, two daggers, two brooches, a knife and toggle pin (with a hollow for fixing to a garment, on which it served as a button to pin the flaps together) and a series of typical late Hyksos scarabs, from Tomb 9. Pages 101, 112.

PLATE XVI. RESIDENCE OF THE LAST KINGS OF JERICHO: AND STORE-ROOMS OF THE HYKSOS PALACE.

a : The excavated ruins of the Royal Palace occupy the forepart of the upper photograph. Behind (L) is the enclosed Spring now called Elisha's Fountain; in the centre the Expedition's drawing office and workshops. Beyond is the cultivated area with the Dead Sea just visible in the background. Pages 8, 30, 117.

b : The lower photograph shows a group of store-rooms of the Hyksos Palace. In Room 45 may be seen a wall fallen to the floor with another falling—effects of the Egyptian assault of 1600 B.C. In Rooms 42 and 44 may be seen the remains of pottery store-vessels as found. Beyond and resting upon this complex (marked m . . . b) are the foundations of the near wall of the later royal residence in the upper photograph of this Plate. Pages 94–96.

PLATE XVII. THE FALLEN WALLS OF CITY IV (1400-1385 B.C.)

a : Section of the wall of City IV partly supported by the older wall of City II. Traces of ash and burnt material on the right ; fissures and dislocation as by earthquake visible in the masonry which is photographed exactly as cleaned by the brush. Pages 34, 111, 134–136.

b : The fallen stone revetment of the outer wall with the brick masonry behind, described in the text in connexion with the diagram on Pl. XVIII. Large stone in the foreground marks the original position of the foundations beyond which the masonry has been projected about 2 ft. Pages 111, 134–136.

PLATE XVIII. THE FALLEN WALLS OF CITY IV (From a Measured Drawing)

B. Brick Wall of the Second City on the Western Scarp.

DD. Walls of the Fourth City.

A measured drawing showing the inner and outer walls of the Fourth City as found. The inner one D rested partly upon the older wall of the Second City B. The revetment to the outer wall has been knocked off its foundations by the impact of falling houses or the upper part of the inner D wall. cf. Plates XII *b* and XVII ; also pages 34, 111, 134–136.

PLATE XIX. GRAIN, DATES AND BREAD FROM A BURNT ROOM OF CITY IV

Among the fruits etc. shown are dates, date stones, an olive and olive stone, an onion, a peppercorn, a piece of bread and a lump of unbaked dough (left), described in the text : page 139.

NOTES ON ILLUSTRATIONS

FIGURES IN THE TEXT

NOTES ON ILLUSTRATIONS

FIG.

20. Late Bronze Age Pottery of City IV: c. 1475 B.C.; page 119.

21. Late Mycenæan Pottery from Tomb 13: these pots came from the upper layer of the re-used tomb; page 123.

22. The Pharaoh as an archer: from a scarab; page 144.

23. Later pottery found outside the limits of the City: Nos. 1-5 (Early Iron Age or transitional) were found in Cremation Pit No. 11 (c. 1200 B.C.), No. 6 is the Late Mycenæan pot found in the fosse (see Fig. 2); pages 123 and 147.

24. Early Iron Age Pottery of City V: c. 800 B.C.; page 149,

INDEX

INDEX

INDEX

INDEX